Drink to Your Health
Did You Know That . . .

Vegetable juice therapy is an ideal way to help you normalize your weight?

A cabbage, carrot, celery and cherry juice combination has been known to help alleviate stomach problems—and even help ulcers?

Carotene-rich fruits and vegetables like carrots, broccoli, apricots, mangoes, pumpkins, squash, sweet potatoes, asparagus, and even dark-leaf lettuce, when juiced, are some of the best cancer-preventatives we have?

Black-cherry juice has been used to treat anemia and gout?

Kale and cabbage juices are high in sulfur, which can be beneficial in diminishing the pain of arthritis?

Prune, apple and pear juices help to alleviate constipation—but so do beet greens, cabbage and spinach?

Cucumber juice is valuable in helping to lower blood pressure and reduce skin eruptions?

Radish juice may help clear up your sinuses?

Total Juicing explains why and how you can treat yourself to delicious juice combinations and excellent health starting today.

• •

ELAINE LaLANNE has used juicing to complement her health-and-fitness lifestyle for many years. She has authored four books and travels extensively with her husband, Jack LaLanne, lecturing and promoting the LaLanne fitness message.

TOTAL

JUICING

*Over 125 Healthful
and Delicious Ways
to Use Fresh Fruit
and Vegetable Juices and Pulp*

ELAINE LALANNE
with Richard Benyo
Introduction by Jack LaLanne

A PLUME BOOK

A NOTE TO THE READER
The ideas, procedures, and suggestions contained in this book are not intended as a substitute for consulting with your physician. All matters regarding your health require medical supervision.

PLUME
Published by the Penguin Group
Penguin Books USA Inc., 375 Hudson Street,
New York, New York 10014, U.S.A.
Penguin Books Ltd, 27 Wrights Lane,
London W8 5TZ, England
Penguin Books Australia Ltd, Ringwood,
Victoria, Australia
Penguin Books Canada Ltd, 10 Alcorn Avenue,
Toronto, Ontario, Canada M4V 3B2
Penguin Books (N.Z.) Ltd, 182–190 Wairau Road,
Auckland 10, New Zealand

Penguin Books Ltd, Registered Offices:
Harmondsworth, Middlesex, England

First published by Plume, an imprint of New American Library, a division of Penguin Books USA Inc.

First Printing, November, 1992

50 49 48 47 46

LIBRARY OF CONGRESS CATALOGING IN PUBLICATION DATA:

ISBN 0-452-26928-8

CIP data available

Printed in the United States of America

Set in Bookman Light

Designed by Stanley S. Drate/Folio Graphics Co. Inc.

Contents

P A R T   O N E

The Art and Science of Juicing

A Walk on the Wild Side
The Unjuiceables

P A R T   T W O

Juicing Recipes

Acknowledgments

I would like to extend my thanks to the following people:

Dr. Gale Shemwell-Rudolph, a Ph.D. in nutrition from UCLA and a consultant in nutrition and food science, for her constructive input in reviewing the manuscript at various stages; Carolyn Katzin, an M.S. in nutrition at the School of Public Health at UCLA, for her invaluable work precisely measuring RDA values of fruits and vegetables to be juiced; Brenda Rodriques, my personal assistant, for her help in finalizing and testing juicing recipes; Rhonda Provost, Giselle Ganes, Denielle Lucas, Chuck Raddleford, and Gloria Rambaud for their creative input in developing new and delicious juice recipes; Jack La-Lanne, who forty years ago convinced me that juicing can, indeed, put the sparkle in your eye—and keep it there; Richard Benyo, my collaborator, who consistently manages to convince me that I've got one more book in me trying to get out, and who one of these days is going to burn out the both of us; and to the friends and acquaintances who were kind enough to share ideas about juicing and their own positive experiences from this fascinating path to good nutrition.

INTRODUCTION

· ·

Nature's Way Is Best

Let's face it: along with fast foods, one of the biggest consumer items in this country, used by almost everyone from the cradle to the grave, is soft drinks. But it is the overconsumption of these foods and so called recreational drinks that can lead to many health problems. And if you're not healthy, it has a negative effect upon your whole life. If you don't feel well, the world around you doesn't feel well. If you don't feel well, you can't enjoy life!

But if you have a healthy body full of energy and vitality, you can have a positive effect on your life—and on your world.

Giving your body the right fuel is just like giving your car the right fuel. If you put gasoline in your car, it will perform for you. But if you put water in the gas tank, the engine will sputter and die.

I believe that if you put live and vital fuel in your God-given body, you're going to feel live and vital.

The way I see the human body is that nature created it in wonderful ways and then turned it over to us to take care of and to improve. Think of your bloodstream as your river of life. If that river is polluted by unhealthy foods, your whole body will be adversely affected. The bloodstream feeds every single cell in your body, over the hundreds of miles of capillaries that function as tributaries of that river of life. The bloodstream brings nourishment to each cell and takes away damaged or dead cells so that they can be excreted. The purity of the bloodstream determines how you look, how you feel, how you ward off disease.

Why do some people age prematurely? Because they have for too long polluted their bloodstream. They have gone against nature's ways. Why do so many people spend so much money on plastic surgery to have their skin tightened? Because they have dumped junk into that river of life and now must pay the price.

If you haven't been eating right, you need to detoxify your bloodstream so that it can once again do the work nature designed it to do.

Besides blemished or pallid skin, nature gives other signs that your bloodstream may be polluted. Hair and nails can indicate trouble: hair can be dull and lifeless with split ends, while nails can break and split easily. You can gloss these problems over by going to the beauty parlor, but they're still there.

The other place where I look to see whether a person's bloodstream is doing its job is the eyes. If a person is living according to nature's way, I see a wonderful gleam in his or her eyes, a vitality that shines out to the world. If a person's eyes are dull and lifeless, I'm sure that his or her river of life is polluted.

The human body is a wonderful machine that was

designed to give us a lot of leeway. You can do many injurious things to yourself, but a few good habits can turn things around.

I've been drinking fresh fruit and vegetable juice since I was fifteen. When I began juicing, my mother was so impressed by the almost instant changes that she wanted to know my secret. I put her on a program similar to mine, which included fresh juice every day. I soon noticed a change: she seemed to come alive, to radiate health. She lived to be ninety-four years old.

You might ask, "Doesn't it take a long time for juice therapy to work?" No, it doesn't. In fact, it begins to work immediately! Fresh juice rushes to your bloodstream. I believe you can see results in a matter of days.

And the wonderful thing is that fresh juices taste delicious. Fresh juice helps normalize your appetite so that you don't crave every unhealthful snack in sight. If you have a weight problem, regularly drinking fresh juice can help stabilize your weight. Fresh juice is filling but not fattening.

Elaine has put together a guide to making fresh juice a part of your life. You won't find *Total Juicing* stuffy or overly scientific—Elaine makes juicing fun. I don't know any bigger fan of the carrot—she just loves it. And I love the twinkle it puts into her eyes. Regular juicing has kept Elaine vital and young, and I know it can do the same for you.

Remember this: it's never too late to start changing your habits. Put fresh juices into your river of life. It's nature's way.

—JACK LALANNE

PREFACE

· ·

The Juicing Revolution

Over the past few years a nutritional revolution has quietly taken place—a revolution made possible by a handful of pioneers in the field of health and fitness.

The juicing revolution came about thanks to a unique technology—a new generation of centrifugal juicing machines that are smaller, less expensive, and easier to clean than cumbersome traditional juicers.

The modern high-speed juicers allow anyone to enjoy the benefits of freshly made juices at home. No more artificially flavored canned or jarred juices sitting on the shelves for months. No more juices from frozen concentrate. No more 10-percent fruit juices. No more vegetable juices to which preservatives and large amounts of salt have been added. No more juices that have been cooked before going into the cans. No more frustration in attempting to find just the right combination of juices to satisfy your very individual taste.

Today, if you can grow fruits or vegetables, or find them in your supermarket's produce section, you can get juice into a glass and into your body in a matter of min-utes. The vitamins, minerals, trace minerals, and other nutrients will still be at the height of their potency. The multitude of benefits available from nature's array of fresh fruits and vegetables is as close to you as the ON switch of your juicer.

This book presents the full spectrum of advantages to your health of drinking fresh juices on a daily basis. It also examines the health benefits from fruits and vege-tables, the vitamin and mineral contents, and ways of combining various fruits and vegetables to maximize those benefits.

I present a variety of recipes that show you how to improve your cooking (and your health) by making use of the pulp that is a by-product from your juicing, but that is often discarded. Pulp is a wonderful storehouse of health-restoring, body-cleansing fiber.

Jack has now been juicing for seven decades. He says: "Juicing can be the fountain of youth that helps you nour-ish your river of life," and he's right.

When I met Jack in the 1950s, he quickly made me a juice convert. I was invited to his home for dinner one evening. I noticed a huge metal contraption in the kitchen. It stood more than twenty inches tall, measured thirty-nine inches around, and weighed sixty pounds.

He said it was a juicer. He proceeded to demonstrate how it worked. With a twenty-five pound bag of carrots, he quickly made a quart of carrot juice. I could not believe how sweet the juice was.

I began to notice a sparkle in the eyes of people at Jack's gym who were drinking juice. I began to notice a sparkle in my own eyes—and I realized that my eyesight had improved, too. Eyes truly mirror the soul, and by looking in a person's eyes, you can gauge his or her level of health. People who regularly drink carrot juice have that healthy sparkle.

There's nothing like a tall glass of freshly made carrot and celery juice to start the morning! There's also nothing like raising your own fruits and vegetables and then juicing them! It's just plain impossible to get anything fresher or better for you than by going out into your garden— whether it covers acres in the country or a window box on the balcony of a city apartment—to pick your own produce, wash it, run it through your juicer, and drink it on the spot. It's the ultimate experience of the word *fresh*.

There are only two areas associated with juicing that this book does not cover: wheatgrass juicing and juice fasting.

Some proponents of juicing are very high on wheatgrass juicing. I agree with them that wheatgrass juicing can be beneficial to your overall health if done judiciously. Unfortunately, wheatgrass cannot be juiced with some of the new high-speed centrifugal juicers; you need a special slow-speed juicer. Since most converts to juicing are coming to the practice by way of the high-tech high-speed centrifugal juicers that are designed specifically for fruits and vegetables, and since juicing fresh fruits and vegetables is the primary form of juicing, this book sticks to fruits and vegetables. For information on wheatgrass juice, try your local health-food store.

On the matter of juice fasting, I must admit that I have fasted, as has Jack, and we have both had satisfactory results. Although it can have very real benefits, fasting should be done only under the supervision of a

professional who is knowledgeable of the demands of fasting—and who is intimate with your medical history. For
some people, fasting may be detrimental. To fast properly
on water or juice, you must follow an entire regimen. It's
important to consult an appropriate practitioner if you
wish to explore this application of fresh juices.

The purpose of this book is to assist the novice and
the veteran juicer in thoroughly enjoying the unique and
delicious tastes of healthful juices, sometimes in new
combinations, and to make fresh juice a valuable supplement to your balanced diet and to your way of life.

So come along with me and learn everything you need
to know to make juicing a part of your life. Raise a glass
and let's salute your good health!

—ELAINE LALANNE
October 1992

PART ONE

THE ART AND
SCIENCE
OF JUICING

1

Juices of Yesterday
and Today

Today, you can go into a grocery store and find shelves full of fruit and vegetable juices. You'll find various-sized cans, bottles, jars, and boxes of tomato, grape, prune, carrot, and apple juices, to name a few. In the frozen foods department, you'll see concentrates of orange, grapefruit, and apple juices, lemonade, and blends of various fruit juices. You'll even find powdered juices.

Refrigerating, quick freezing, canning, and dehydrating juices into powders are conveniences of the modern world that put almost every imaginable juice at our fingertips. But all of the processing involved in lengthening the shelf life of juices has a negative effect on its nutritional value.

In rural America of a hundred years ago, the grape and the apple press were standard tools on the farm. From the time July apples became ripe until the last apples of fall matured, apples were pressed for their fresh juices. The same press was used for pears and other fruits. Later, almost every home had a citrus juicer for squeezing the fresh juice from oranges and grapefruits. You can still find these basic citrus juicers at the antiques shops and even in some small-town hardware stores.

In years past, many country doctors prescribed freshly squeezed carrot or cabbage juice for stomach ulcers. The country doctor also used to recommend cabbage juice for weight loss and regularity. Today we know that those old doctors were far ahead of their time—fresh carrot and cabbage juice offer a wide range of benefits.

Gradually, and then with increasing speed, refrigerators and supermarkets overtook the icebox and the corner grocery store, and streamlined food processing made it seem silly to work so hard for a glass of carrot, orange, or tomato juice. Besides, the processing plant could add that extra touch of sugar to grapefruit juice to satisfy our growing national sweet tooth, or add that shot of salt to tomato juice to quiet our increasing addiction to salt in store-bought foods. Squeezing your own juices was old-fashioned, and old-fashioned was "out."

"Progress" has taken away that instant and complete connection with the source of the fruit or vegetable farm—and an excellent source of good health and well-being—by placing a processing plant between us.

A Look Behind the Scenes

If you could go to a processing plant and stand by a spigot at the crushing tanks with your glass, you would get a fairly fresh glass of juice. If you stood at the far end of the processing line—sometimes in an entirely different factory—the liquid that would pour into your glass would probably be hot. It would contain additives and preservatives to maintain color or to increase its shelf life.

As soon as a fresh fruit or vegetable is turned into juice, the process of deterioration begins. If a day passes between the juicing and the canning or jarring, the vitamin and mineral content of the juice can be (almost) halved. Even the ripest, most delicious fruits and vegetables suffer during processing.

When you read the label on a container of processed juice, you'll often see that ascorbic acid has been added: the natural vitamin C has been destroyed by heating, or by the wait to be processed, and the factory has attempted to put some back. The loss of vitamins doesn't stop with the processing, either. The longer the product sits on the store shelves or in your pantry, the more vitamins and minerals are lost.

One additive that frequently goes into juices (especially vegetable juices) is salt. We *could* get more than our daily requirement of sodium just from eating fresh fruits and vegetables. Vegetables such as spinach, celery, beets, turnips, and kale have quite a bit of natural sodium to start with. But the typical American is overdosed with salt, and two-thirds of the salt in the usual American diet comes from packaged foods. This problem is further complicated by the fact that bottling and canning increase the sodium content of vegetables dramatically, at the same time decreasing the content of vital potassium. Potassium is essential for maintaining soft tissue and plays a major role in controlling the negative effects of sodium on the body.

Home Juicing Makes Dollars and Sense

You don't fire up a processing plant on a whim. The energy needed to heat the fruit and vegetable juices during the processing is costly, and so is the packaging—not to mention the advertising needed to get people to buy the product. The company must make a profit, so all of these costs must be passed along to the consumer. We pay dearly for the convenience of convenience foods.

But you can simply walk down the produce aisle and fill your cart with fresh fruits and vegetables and then take them home, juice them, and drink them within minutes! There's no heating process to rob the fruits and vegetables of vitamins and minerals, there's no shelf life to worry about—everything the food in its natural state has to offer goes directly into you and immediately gets to work. And, you spend a fraction of the amount you would have for packaged, processed juice.

Which Juicer Is Right for You?

Many types of juicers are available today, from low-speed wheatgrass juicers to masticating juicers, from manual juicers to centrifugal juicers. It all sounds more confusing than it is. Let's very briefly look at several types of machines.

Wheatgrass juicers. These juicers are designed to extract juice from sprouts, greens, and wheatgrass, members of the vegetable family that do not contain much juice to begin with. Wheatgrass juicers turn very slowly and use a blade to squeeze the juice from such vegetable matter. This is the only type of juicer that can be used for grasses.

Masticating juicers. Masticating is what we do with our food when we chew it. A masticating juicer does much the same thing—it crushes the fruits and vegetables and then, by squeezing the crushed mass with tremendous pressure, it produces juice. You'll find two basic categories of masticating juicers: the basic type, which crushes the fruits or vegetables into a paste and then squeezes out the juice, and the masticating juicer with a hydraulic press, which sends the paste to a bag from which the juice is squeezed out. These juicers tend to produce more juice per pound of food.

The juicers that have figured primarily in the juicing revolution are the *centrifugal juicers.* These juicers (with or without pulp ejectors) have a high-speed continuous blade/separator at the top. You cut your fruits and vegetables to size and press them into a slot at the top; they hit the high-speed stainless-steel grater edges inside the strainer basket and are immediately separated into juice and pulp. The centrifugal juicer with pulp extractor sends the juice into one container and the pulp into another.

This centrifugal juicer with pulp extractor (or ejector) is the one I use and the one that is most popular today. It allows for easy juicing and provides a ready source of fresh pulp for other recipes. Such a juicer costs from around $30 to $250 at a department store, at an appliance store, or through the mail.

It's worth your while to ask about the guarantee that goes along with any juicer you purchase, and to ask about the ease of repair and part replacement. If you're going to use your juicer daily, it will obviously get quite a workout.

A few extra dollars for a high-quality machine should ensure many years of juicing.

Caring for Your Juicer

There are some basic habits you'll want to get into to keep your juicer in the best operating condition:

1. When you purchase your machine, read the manual carefully. Take a few minutes to get to know the machine and its parts.

2. Before juicing any fruits or vegetables, thoroughly wash the machine's removable parts according to the manual. If the instructions say you can run the parts through your dishwasher, do so. Always place the parts in the upper rack of the dishwasher, however, so that they do not warp in the heat from the drying element at the bottom. Do not lay the machine parts out on the prongs that stick up from the dishwasher shelves; vibration may cause the prongs to damage the parts. Some manufacturers do not recommend washing the parts of the machine in a dishwasher, due to the tendency of the extreme heat to warp some plastic parts. If this is the case, wash the parts in warm, soapy water and rinse thoroughly.

3. I strongly recommend that once you've used your machine, before you place the blade element in the dishwasher or wash it by hand, you hold it under warm water and use a vegetable brush to get the particles of fruit and vegetable matter out of the basket holes.

4. Always clean the parts of your machine as soon after juicing as possible to avoid the growth of bacteria.

5. Dry the parts before you put the juicer back together.

6. Store your juicer as you do any other small appliance. If you also have a high-speed blender on your counter, you might want to store them side by side, since some recipes (such as those which include bananas) call for the quick use of a blender. If you're not going to use your juicer for several days, protect it with a plastic or cloth cover.

7. Always keep your juicer unplugged until you're ready to use it, especially if you have children in the house.

8. Always use your juicer on a flat, hard surface. Before starting it up, make certain that all the parts are fitted together snugly and that the rubber or plastic legs are planted firmly. This will minimize vibration and lengthen your juicer's life.

9. Clean any vegetable discoloration (such as the orange from carrots) off your juicer with a scouring pad or scouring powder.

Getting the Most from Your Investment

You can get the most from your centrifugal juicer with pulp extractor *by making juice and then using the pulp as a primary fiber source in a variety of other recipes.*

Some people who juice advise you to use the pulp in your compost heap. For the pulp from certain vegetables, that's a good idea. But most of the pulp you produce from your juicer is a source of important natural fiber, as you'll see in Part 2 of this book. Carrot pulp, for example, can be used for carrot cake; the pulp of tomatoes, onions, garlic, and bell peppers can be used for salsas or pasta sauce; the pulp of apples is instant applesauce.

So Economy Rule #1 is: Make use of the pulp whenever possible.

Economy Rule #2 is: Buy in season. If it's apple season and you can find inexpensive apples in your produce section or at a roadside stand, turn the month into a festival of apples and juice apples as often as is practical. You can vary the taste and consistency of the apple juice by adding other fruits—berries are especially good.

Economy Rule #3: Watch for specials and for quick-sale items that are a day or two past their prime. Red bell peppers, for example, are generally much more expensive than green bell peppers, but they're much sweeter and are a real treat to juice when you can find them priced right. And don't forget to recycle the pulp as an ingredient for salsa.

Economy Rule #4: Buy in bulk. A basket of apples or potatoes is less expensive than a handful bought individually.

Economy Rule #4A: Go in with neighbors and friends to buy in bulk. You may be able to get some real deals at your produce section if you form a juicing club and buy apples or carrots (the two prime juice ingredients) in large enough amounts to make it economically feasible for the greengrocer to accommodate you.

Storing Fresh Juices

Every growing thing in this world has its one golden moment in the sun—that moment at which everything is at its maximum of ripeness, its zenith of fulfillment, its apex of power.

If you regularly shop in a fruit and vegetable market or if you have a garden, you know that this is true of fruits and vegetables.

Take apples, for instance. A certain day arrives when—although the apple will still be good for several weeks—it is obviously at its height and should, under ideal circumstances, be picked and eaten.

Fruits and vegetables, of course, have different windows of ripeness. In general, the denser a fruit or vegetable, the longer it can hold its ripeness. An apple will hold its ripeness many days longer than a basket of blackberries. And some apples hold their ripeness much longer than others. The Gravenstein, which is excellent for making apple pies and applesauce, doesn't keep very long, while a Golden Delicious has an extended shelf life.

Among vegetables, carrots, which are quite dense, will stay fresh much longer than a head of iceberg lettuce.

One factor that determines how long a fruit or vegetable will stay fresh once it ripens is the way it is stored. Heat hastens the ripening—and the rotting—process, while cold generally retards it.

There is simply no way to get more of the vital vitamins, minerals, and trace elements from fruits or vegetables than to eat them straight from the garden. Every minute the fruit or vegetable is away from where it was grown, its vital ingredients deteriorate. The longer the fruit or vegetable is away from its source, the faster the deterioration proceeds.

We can certainly understand why bunches of bananas are picked while they are still green for shipment from Central and South America to the United States. If they were picked when they were ripe, by the time they made the trip here in the holds of ships, they'd be brown, mushy messes.

For all practical purposes, the fruits and vegetables you buy will have begun the process of losing vitamins and minerals. But with the tremendous advances that have been made in shipping methods over the past century, you can buy fruits and vegetables that are as fresh as is reasonable. And it's what you do with them once you bring them home that, to a large extent, determines just how much benefit you get from them.

Ideally, you should shop every day for produce, but the vegetable crisper in the refrigerator does help extend the useful life of the produce, and helps hold in the vitamins and minerals.

When you make fresh juice, you should take the fruits and/or vegetables you're going to use, wash them, dry them, and juice them immediately.

And you should immediately drink the juice—while it is at its peak of freshness and potency. I don't mean that you should gulp it down, but you should drink the juice within fifteen or twenty minutes of having juiced it. Even that amount of time allows the juice to lose some of its potency.

But, people tell me, it's such a chore to make a glass of fresh juice, drink it, then clean the juicer, and then have to do it all over again in a few hours when they want another glass.

I'm afraid that if you want your fresh juice at its peak, that's exactly how you need to do it. Fortunately, most of the modern juicers are very easy to disassemble, clean, and reassemble. You can do it in a matter of minutes.

I wish I could say that you should make two quarts of juice first thing in the morning, put it in a pitcher, and keep it in the refrigerator for use during the day. Certainly, you *can* do that, but as the day wears on, the juice will lose significant amounts of vitamins and trace elements. And some juices—especially cabbage—will become quite foul, which is an indication of just how fragile fresh juices are.

Some juices lend themselves better to storage for a few hours. Carrot juice stays quite well, as do apple and orange juice, but even though they retain their good taste, you must understand that once they are juiced, they lose vitality by the minute. Within twenty-four hours, for example, carrot juice can lose fully half of its vitamins, minerals, and trace elements. Within twenty-four hours, cabbage juice will become so rank as to chase you out of the house when you open the refrigerator door.

If you are willing to sacrifice some of the vitality of the fresh juice for the convenience of having the juice waiting for you in the refrigerator, store it in a covered container. Fresh juice is best stored in glass; plastic can cause a slight alteration in taste.

You can use a pint or quart mason jar with a screw top to keep your juice as fresh as possible. Use the smallest size that will hold the juice; the air that is trapped inside the jar with the juice will work to deteriorate its good effects, so you want as little air as possible.

There are some fruits and vegetables you do not want to store for later use once they are juiced. Besides cabbage, they include lettuce (which begins to ferment quickly once juiced), greens, potatoes, Jerusalem artichokes, onions, garlic, mangoes, papayas, many of the berries, cherries, and several of the melons.

Fruit and vegetable juices that stay relatively fresh-tasting if chilled in a covered container are apple, grape, citrus, peach, pear, prune, kiwi, pineapple, beet, carrot, and celery.

You can help your fruit and vegetable juices hold their flavor by adding a few drops of fresh lemon juice per ounce.

Another alternative you might want to consider, especially if you want to extend the period during which you can enjoy fresh juices from seasonal fruits and vegetables, is to make the juice, add a few drops of fresh lemon per ounce, and *immediately* freeze it in sealable plastic containers. Freeze only juices that have a longer life to begin with. Don't bother attempting to freeze some of the juices that deteriorate quickly, because when you add the amount of time it takes to freeze and then to thaw the juice, the total is just too much to keep the juice drinkable. Naturally, do not keep fresh juices frozen for more than several weeks—even frozen, they will begin to go bad.

In the final analysis, the beauty of the new high-tech juicers is that they make it much more convenient to make *fresh* juice at a moment's notice.

Dos and Don'ts

DO buy your fruits and vegetables when they are at the height of their ripeness and juice them immediately for the greatest benefit.

DON'T store your fruits and vegetables when they are at the height of their ripeness.

DO buy your fruits and vegetables when they have a few days to go before they reach maximum ripeness if you do not plan to use them immediately.

DON'T make more juice than you are going to drink immediately. If you do make more than you can drink, store the remainder in a sealed glass jar and place it in the refrigerator.

DON'T store juices such as cabbage juice for more than an hour or two. You'll understand why you don't want to if you happen to do so by accident.

DON'T store juice in a glass container that is too large because the air trapped inside will deteriorate the juice.

DO clean your juicer *immediately* after using it so that it is ready to go when you have the urge to make more juice.

DON'T freeze juice for any longer than a month.

DO enjoy fresh juice at least once a day.

2

Juicing for Your Health

The most perfect formula for good health is this: A Well-Balanced Diet + Moderate Aerobic Exercise. Unfortunately, too many people get too little exercise and most people do not have a balanced diet.

If you exercise regularly and have a less-than-perfect diet you will be more healthy than if you have an excellent diet and never exercise. Exercise is an essential ingredient of life. Our bodies were designed to move, not to sit. When we accept a sedentary lifestyle, we throw away a good deal of our existence, because from the neck on down we become dead.

The wonderful thing about exercise and the human body is that a little bit goes a long way. You don't have to run marathons to see marvelous results. If you walk briskly for an hour a day you will see your body reshape itself into a leaner, meaner machine that will be better able to make efficient use of all the good foods and juices you are using to fuel yourself.

The Search for the Balanced Diet

We have been seeing news about the government's attempts to make it easier for people to understand what constitutes a balanced diet. Whether or not you choose to follow the four basic food groups, your diet should include a mix of meat or meat alternatives, dairy products, fruits and vegetables, and enriched or whole-grain breads and cereals.

Juice—The Ultimate Supplement

What makes juicing so exciting is that literally millions of people are now enjoying and benefiting from the tremendous storehouse of vitamins, minerals, and trace elements available in fresh fruits and vegetables. From a health standpoint, that is very exciting.

1. By juicing you reap the benefits of taking nature's vitamins and minerals direct and unaltered.
2. By juicing the all-important enzymes are released, and these enzymes benefit the human machine on so many different levels.
3. By juicing fresh fruits and vegetables you fill yourself up with good nutrition and cut down on the ingestion of fatty foods.

By juicing at least once a day, you provide your body with a fresh, vital source of vitamins and minerals that serve to *supplement* your regular diet. Juicing should never substitute for a balanced diet of nutritious solid foods.

Fresh Juice as a Detoxifier

We are all constantly absorbing toxins from the air we breathe, the air that touches our skin, the water we drink, the water in which we swim and bathe, often the food we eat. Fortunately, the human body is a tough and adaptable organism. It works hard to rid itself of toxins in a variety of ways.

We get rid of toxins by excreting them in both our stool and our urine. We also rid ourselves of toxins when we perspire, which is one reason regular exercise is good for us.

The major problem with the toxins we absorb from the world around us is that they counter our ability to store and use essential vitamins and minerals. In very large doses, these toxins can actually undermine and sometimes destroy vital body functions.

Let's take a moment to examine:

- common sources of toxins.
- problems those toxins create for us.
- how regular juicing can work not only to rid us of the toxins, but to fill us with vitality and good health by fortifying our body systems with essential vitamins, minerals, and trace elements.

Did you know that the place where you're most likely to find toxins is indoors? That's right. "Indoors" includes your home, at your office, and at the stores where you shop.

We all know about the dangers of certain kinds of asbestos, the material that for years was used as insulation. But asbestos is not the only toxic material that should concern us. Other kinds of insulation can be toxic if absorbed in certain amounts. Many cleaning products can be toxic when absorbed over a long period. Even certain perfumes and fragrances, if used to excess, can build up as toxins within the body. The same is true of accumulated dust. If you've ever watched the demolition of an old house, you've seen clouds of decades-old dust rise into the air when the house falls. The inhabitants breathed in that dust for as long as they lived in the house.

Right now you can march up to a cache of toxins merely by opening the cupboard door under the sink where you store your cleaning and drain-clearing materials. In too strong a concentration, these chemicals can negatively affect your health.

In office buildings that use central air-conditioning, the recirculated air can build up toxins as it passes insulation and circuit breakers and stored chemicals and works its way through filters that may not have been replaced as often as they should have been. They even have a name these days for the negative physical effects on people in such buildings: sick-building syndrome.

And then there are our bodies!

Toxins build up in our bodies on a regular basis, especially when we overindulge. Did you drink too much alcohol last night? Your kidneys and liver must work overtime to attempt to filter out the toxins, but the organs cannot rid the body of all the toxins at one time; many of them accumulate to dangerous levels. Did you overeat within the last week? Your body must work overtime to attempt to process all that food, and must process not only the toxins in the food you ate, but also the toxins which the body itself pours out as it overworks. To complicate this, we often eat foods that do not easily pass through our bodies, such as fatty meats.

The human body is a marvelous machine, though, and given a little help, it can usually handle almost every toxin it is likely to encounter. According to recent studies, a whole roster of symptoms appear as the body attempts to rid itself of toxic buildups. You may suffer headaches and sleep disturbances, upset stomach, and loose bowels; you may be easily tired, or experience gassiness (both flatulence and a tendency to belch), difficulty in concentrating for more than a few minutes, back pain, skin problems (dry and flaky skin, pallor, blotches), unexplained aches and pains in your extremities, and difficulty breathing.

The best way to flush the toxins from the body is to drink plenty of water and plenty of fresh fruit and vegetable juices!

Each cell of the body has a specific function: liver cells process toxins from the body, cells in the lungs exchange waste gases for fresh oxygen. Our cells are constantly in the process of doing their jobs, and when they are worn out, they are replaced. Every cell in your body changes every sixty to ninety days except for your central nervous system. This constant replacement process in itself rids us of a certain number of toxins.

Our cells can do their job best if they are bathed in fluid. Just like the parts of a car's motor, which work best when they are bathed in oil, so your own cells function best when they are well hydrated.

We do not always give our bodies enough fluid each day in the form of water and juices. We've all heard that we need to drink at least eight glasses of water a day, but many people don't. Some people think they'll gain weight from all that water. This, of course, is incorrect. If we drink enough water and juices each day, we can actually stabilize our weight and sometimes even lose pounds, because processing the fluid in the body flushes everything through, ridding us of excess and detrimental materials.

Pure water is an excellent fluid to take each day. But plain water has a basic shortcoming. It does not bring any fresh nourishment to the cells and the body's organs. Certain toxins can have a devastating effect on the body's ability to store, receive, and process certain vitamins and minerals. For instance, too much alcohol breaks down the B vitamins. A daily treat of freshly squeezed fruit and vegetable juices helps rid your body of toxins and provides the nourishment it needs.

Daily juicing:

- provides needed fluid to the cells.
- flushes toxins from the cells.
- replaces expended vitamins and minerals.
- builds up a store of vitamins and minerals that can be called up by the body as needed.
- assists with regular bowel movements and, by assuring regularity and regular urine production, rids the body of waste materials that, if retained, can lead to cancer and other diseases.

Fresh fruit and vegetable juices speed relief to the body. When you consume fruits and vegetables in pure juice form, the stomach can more readily process the vitamins, minerals, and fluids while using less of the body's energy, since the juicer has already done much of the stomach's work for it by breaking the fruits and vegetables down into a more easily digestible form.

There is no way we can escape continuing exposure to toxins. They are all around us. And, for the most part, the body is ready and willing to break down and excrete the majority of toxins we encounter in our daily life. But our bodies need our help not only in breaking down and flushing out the toxins, but in replacing the depleted vitamins and minerals.

Best Juice Recipes for Detoxification

. . . .

Sunrise-Sunset (page 103)

Blackberry Apple Delight (page 107)

The Lunch Bucket (page 122)

Potato Power (page 137)

Sweet Deluxe (page 143)

A Note on Diet

The speed with which home juicing is catching on concerns me because some people substitute juices for a balanced diet. Fresh fruit and vegetable juices are not to be used as a sole source of nutrition—they should *only* be used to supplement your balanced diet. Ignoring solid food is ill-advised at best, and can be seriously detrimental.

One reason that this book contains a section on cooking and baking with pulp is that the juicing process extracts the fiber from the fresh fruits and vegetables, and your body needs fiber to function well.

Body systems, just like muscles, must be exercised in order to remain strong. If you don't vigorously chew solid food on a regular basis, you may suffer from weakened muscles in the jaw and face. Your stomach needs to work regularly on solid food, or it, too, can become weak and less able to digest foods properly. It is very important to your general overall health to regularly move fecal matter through the intestines and colon. If you don't do this, you invite a variety of problems into your digestive tract.

So let's make it very clear: fresh juices are meant to *supplement* a balanced diet of solid foods, and should never be used as a substitute.

Fresh Juice and Weight Loss

When I talk about diet, I like to make clear that I mean "balanced diet." When I speak of weight control, I like to think in terms of "a way of life," and "a way of life" is something you practice *regularly*, just like daily exercise. If you look at your diet as a way of life rather than as a quick fix for excess body weight, you'll lose weight and keep it off as part of who and what you are. And if you can think in those terms, you will no longer be obsessed with food and with dieting.

It was no real news to me when in April 1992 a blue-ribbon panel of experts at the National Institutes of

Health announced, in chairwoman Dr. Suzanne
Fletcher's words, "Most people who need to lose weight are
not succeeding." The figures presented were staggering:

- Some 25 million Americans are overweight.
- At any given time in America, one-third of all adult
  women and one-fourth of all adult men are attempting to lose weight.
- Even after going through the best commercial
  weight-reduction programs, 95 percent of people
  regain the weight within five years. As many as two-
  thirds of these people regain the weight *within the
  first year.*

What were the recommendations of the twelve-mem-
ber panel? The same recommendations Jack and I have
been making for years as we speak to groups of
Americans:

Instead of setting a specific, short-term weight-loss
target, adopt a longer view, a way of life that emphasizes:

1. a healthier lifestyle.
2. exercise.
3. dietary changes.
4. thinking svelte.
5. instead of being positive about the words "I can't,"
   being positive about the words "I can."

In other words, go on a "diet" that's a "way of life," be
patient, and your dreams of a healthier, happier, slimmer
self will come true.

One of the most effective—and one of the healthiest—

changes you can make in your life for the purpose of losing excess body weight is to juice on a regular basis.

I want to stress again that juicing should not be used as a substitute for a balanced diet, but to complement it.

How, then, can you use juicing to reduce your weight? Here is a simple, easy-to-follow method.

At least one meal per day should be a solid, well-balanced, sit-down, take-your-time-eating-it meal. This sit-down meal—and it can be breakfast, lunch or dinner, whichever is more convenient—should be of sensible portions and should be prepared in a healthful manner: low in fat and high in carbohydrates, including fresh vegetables (lightly cooked or in the form of a salad with low-fat dressing, or both). Before you sit down to eat your main meal, drink a big glass of water. This will help fill you so that you will not have the urge to overeat.

Open enough time in your life that you can enjoy your main meal. Attempt to eat it under calm, peaceful conditions. Make yourself a half glass of fresh vegetable juice and add water to fill the glass to the top; this allows you to cut down the total calories for the day while also assuring that you get your needed water. Eat your meal slowly. Chew thoroughly and savor your food. Sip your vegetable juice between bites. This too will help fill you up.

By taking your time you're doing a couple of good things for yourself: you are *gradually* feeding food to your stomach, so that it does not have to pump out stomach acids to process the food (this also helps prevent the formation of stomach ulcers) and you are limiting the amount of food you eat to sensible portions. The body has a regulating apparatus that tells you when you have had enough food to eat. It takes only a few minutes after you begin eating for the message to travel from your stomach to your brain. If you eat too fast during those few minutes, you will eat enough calories on a daily basis to keep yourself fat for the rest of your life—on food that your stomach really didn't want. By eating slowly, you give your stomach time to send the signal to your brain that it is filled and doesn't need any more food, thank you very much. You can save yourself hundreds of calories a day and a great deal of money over a longer period, because you will find that smaller portions are just as satisfying as larger ones used to be.

Now, after your main meal, I have a suggestion for you: put thirty to forty-five minutes aside and go out for a brisk walk. In that time you can cover several miles, which means that you will burn up several hundred additional calories, while also improving your cardiovascular health and building muscle tone.

What about the other meals during the day?

Unless your doctor tells you that you need solid food on a regular basis, you can drink some of your other meals by creating delicious, healthful vegetable juice combinations. (You should, however, eat something solid with your morning juice.) I recommend that you drink primarily vegetable juices, since they are filled with essential vitamins and minerals and are lower in sugar (and therefore calories) than fruit juices. When you drink your juiced vegetables, add water (a 50/50 proportion is best, but if you think that thins out the taste of the juice too much, go 60/40 or 70/30 in favor of the juice). You can spice up the blander vegetable juices by adding apple juice to taste.

You can certainly have one glass of fruit juice cut with water a day, but by and large, you are better off using vegetable juices. Of the common vegetables, the better ones for purposes of weight control are beets, cabbage, and carrots. When you do drink fruit juices, don't overdo it with citrus; the acidity can eventually upset the stomach if the citrus juices are not combined with those of other fruits. The best and most easily juiced fruits are apples, melons, and grapes.

Drink those eight glasses of water a day. As we've explained, your body needs a constant supply of water for digestion and other organ functions, for distributing vital nutrients, for removing waste, and for cooling. "The kidneys get rid of toxic metabolites in the body," says Dr. Richard Powell, an endocrinologist and bariatrician (weight-loss specialist) from Santa Rosa, California. "They have to work overtime if they don't get enough water. If the kidneys can't handle the toxic substances, you get a high level [of toxins] in the blood. Then the liver has to do it, and can't metabolize fat as well."

Additionally, a lack of water triggers the production of a hormone that causes salt retention. Drinking enough water washes the excess salts out of the body. Also, if the urine is chronically concentrated (which is what happens when you consume too little water), calcium, oxalates, and other minerals may crystallize into stones rather than being flushed out of the system.

The way to tell whether you're drinking enough water is not by your level of thirst, because when you become thirsty, it's a sign that you are already very much behind in meeting your water needs. Stephanie Karras, a dietitian at the Petaluma Valley Hospital in California, puts it this way: "If you drink only when you're thirsty, you'll only get about fifty percent of the fluids your body needs. We're not in tune with our thirst signals."

Best Juice Recipes for Weight Loss

. . . .

Breakfast Treat (page 103)

Vitamin C Punch (page 106)

Berry Blizzard (page 107)

Breakfast Punch (page 108)

Up and At 'Em (page 109)

Weight Gain Through Juicing

There are some people who struggle all their lives to *gain* weight while most of us continue to attempt to drop it.

If you're naturally slim, count your blessings. Statistically, you will live longer than the heavier person, and you'll never have to wrestle with the psychological problems associated with being overweight.

My primary recommendation for gaining weight is to go onto an exercise program that will build muscle tissue. Remember: exercise is a body normalizer. This makes you healthier while also contouring your body attractively.

As far as your eating and drinking habits go, stay away from fatty foods—although such foods add calories, they aren't calories that improve your health. Eat a diet that leans heavily toward the complex carbohydrates: pastas, lots of potatoes, rice, lentils, dates, nuts, dried fruits (especially raisins), and plenty of fresh vegetables.

As for juicing, drink juices made from fruits that have more calories, like pineapples, grapes, cherries, berries, and the tropical fruits, like papayas, mangoes, and passion fruit.

About a half hour before you eat, drink water or juice flavored with fresh lemon; lemon tends to stimulate the appetite.

It's possible to drink more than you would normally eat, so you *can* manage to consume enough calories to put on weight if you drink five or six big glasses of fresh juice a day. Don't cut the juice with water, as I've advised for the weight-loss program, but do make certain you drink your eight to ten glasses of juice and water a day. Certainly, the more active you are—especially in the summer—the more fluids you should drink.

If you want to gain weight fairly quickly, mix some protein powder in with your juices.

Best Juice Recipes for Weight Gain
. . . .

Pineapple Zip (page 132)

Triple Grape Juice (page 134)

Carrot-Cake Juice (page 135)

Pineapple Turbo (page 153)

Fruity Banana Split (page 231)

Fresh Juice—High-Octane Fuel for Any Age or Energy Level

There are two groups of people in this country who do not get sufficient vitamins and minerals and who usually suffer from lack of a balanced diet: the young and the old.

Energy and the Young

The younger person tends to avoid good food and gravitate toward junk, while the older person, for a variety of reasons, doesn't go to the trouble of preparing a well-balanced meal. Juicing is a solution for both.

JUICE RECOMMENDATIONS

Fruit-based juices are excellent for energetic young people because they contain both complex carbohydrates and simple sugars. Simple sugars give a quick energy boost by causing an insulin reaction—but that quick energy drops off rapidly, leaving the body more tired than before. Simple sugars can be found in soft drinks, where they are often joined by caffeine, and in candy bars.

Although fruit juices have simple sugars, they also contain plenty of complex carbohydrates, which take longer to be processed. Their energy effects stretch out over a longer period.

Fruit juices offer another benefit to the young person who is not following a balanced diet and who, in fact, regularly eats foods that are less than nutritious. Freshly juiced fruits contain certain acids which have the ability both to clean the system of certain toxins and to help kill various bacteria.

The first fruit acid you probably think of is citric acid,

which is most common in citrus fruits. This acid is helpful in flushing waste from the body as well as destroying certain types of bacteria. Orange juice, which most people prefer, is terrific as a source of fluid, and the vitamin C it contains is excellent for the body's defenses against germs. Younger people, with their higher metabolisms, are much better at digesting orange juice's citric acid. Citric acid is also present in cranberries, strawberries, raspberries, and other types of berries.

A second fruit acid is tartaric acid, present in grapes and to some extent in pineapples, and very effective as an antibacterial agent. A third is malic acid, valuable for keeping the major abdominal organs—the stomach, intestines, and liver—clean and functioning. Malic acid is common in apples, bananas, cherries, peaches, plums, apricots, and prunes.

An excellent energy drink for a young person might be a 12- to 16-ounce mixture of pineapple, grapes, oranges, strawberries, and peaches. Try to mix some fruit from each of the three acid groups.

Best Juice Recipes for Young People

. . . .

Vitamin C Punch (page 106)

Vital C Punch (page 118)

The Vitamin Whiz (page 128)

Melontasia (page 131)

Orangeade (page 145)

Juicing for Older People

The older person usually has one of two responses to the slowing of the metabolism that comes with aging: he or she eats less food to accommodate the lower requirements, or continues to eat at the same rate as always, which results in added body fat. Either reaction can cause problems.

If you cut back your consumption of food, you avoid gaining weight. However, you also limit the amount and variety of important vitamins and minerals that you take in. This is why Jack and I frequently recommend that older people supplement their diets with multivitamin and mineral supplements.

At the other extreme is the person who continues to eat the same way as before even though his or her metabolic furnace has been damped down. The excess calories turn to fat, which is more difficult to get rid of the older you become.

Both those who've cut back their caloric intake and those who haven't experience frequent energy lapses during the average day. In the first instance, the lapses come because the person is not getting enough nutritious food to meet minimum needs. In the second instance, the person is battling excess body weight, which robs the body of a tremendous amount of energy.

JUICE RECOMMENDATIONS
For both types of older individuals, fresh juice makes sense. I recommend carrot and apple juices. Older people do not need more orange juice or other citrus juice; too much citrus, for the elderly, tends to make the blood too

acid, and to balance itself out, the body shifts alkaline
minerals from other parts of the body, such as bones.
Just at the time of life when a person's bones need all the
calcium they can get in order to prevent osteoporosis, too
much citric acid can take it away from them in an effort
to achieve an acid/alkaline balance.

I highly recommend that older people start any fruit-
juice energy drink with apples, for several reasons: apples
can ease arthritis and rheumatism and flush out the kidneys and liver, and they are low in calories. They are also
generally inexpensive compared to other fruits.

So, start with apples, cut them into quarters or
eighths, and process them through the juicer. Then fill
out the flavor with melons, pears, cherries, peaches, papaya (if you can find them on sale), a few strawberries (if
they're in season), and perhaps even a quince. Experiment with different mixtures, but go lightly on the citrus.
Make yourself an 8- to 12-ounce glass for a midafternoon
picker-upper. If you use the apple as your base fruit, you'll
get both simple sugars and complex carbohydrates, as
well as a spectrum of vitamins and minerals with a minimum of calories.

I can't recommend carrot juice enough as the universal juice. It has everything going for it. It's high in beta-
carotene, which helps fight cancer, and is extremely rich
in many essential vitamins and minerals. The additional
benefit of carrot juice is that when it is juiced, it becomes
very sweet and can be readily mixed with fruit juices. Why
not make yourself a cocktail of apple *and* carrot juice?

Best Juice Recipes for Seniors

. . . .

Morning Delight (page 102)

Pineapple-Pear Zing (page 104)

Pine-Straw Juice (page 133)

Raspberry Rush (page 154)

Mango Joe (page 156)

The Challenge of the Sedentary

For the sedentary person of any age, there is a tendency toward decline. The sedentary person eats normal amounts of food but does not burn off any of the excess, so he or she is likely to become overweight. The cardiovascular system remains unchallenged and the body becomes sluggish. The foods that *are* consumed take a long time to move through the body, which causes discomfort along the entire digestive tract.

Sedentary people do not want to hear that they should begin a modest exercise program, but that is the case. Everyone needs to exercise in order to raise the metabolism and burn off excess fat while challenging the cardiovascular system to prevent diseases of the heart and blood vessels.

JUICE RECOMMENDATIONS

Use the apple as your base and expand from there. Again, the apple is relatively inexpensive, contains plenty of fluid, offers a variety of vitamins and minerals (vitamin A, several Bs [including B9, or folic acid], C, biotin, and pantothenic acid, as well as phosphorus, manganese, chlorine, copper, magnesium, potassium, silicon, iron, sodium, sulfur, and more), and is low in calories. What kinds of fruit can you add to the apple? Watermelon for lots of beneficial fluid with few calories, and cranberries, grapes, oranges, and prunes to help end irregularity, which is often a problem among sedentary people. How much fresh fruit juice? If you are forty years old or younger and are sedentary, drink 12 to 16 ounces midway through the afternoon as an energy supplement; if you are over forty, cut it back to 8 or 12 ounces in consideration of your lower metabolism. When you drink your energy drink, you might want to follow it with an equal volume of water. This will help fill you up, and will help quiet your appetite while extending the good effects of the complex sugars in the fruit juice.

Carrot juice is beneficial to the sedentary person because it has been shown to be effective in heading off certain types of cancer. Sedentary people tend toward overweight, and overweight can lead to certain cancers. Follow the advice above about apple juice for the amount of carrot juice to drink midafternoon. Of course, you can get the benefits of both juices by blending them.

Best Juice Recipes for Recharging Energy

· ·

Fuel for the Active Body

When a person is physically active, the metabolic process is regulated by the individual instead of by the arbitrary dictates of aging. If you become physically active, your body responds by turning up the metabolic furnace's thermostat. The increased activity requires the body to burn more calories, either from excess body fat or from additional food. The benefit of this process is twofold: your body weight drops because your activity burns up excess weight, and by eating extra food to fuel your activity, you provide for your body a wider variety of necessary vitamins and minerals. But besides that, the active body can make fuller use of the vitamins and minerals it takes in.

JUICE RECOMMENDATIONS

For the active person, fruit-based juices are best. Because of the large caloric output, the active person can afford to drink just about any kind of fruit juice he or she wants. He or she can safely use more of the citrus juices because they will be metabolized better, even if the active person is older. The ideal drink for the active person looking for quick *and sustained* energy begins—once again—with the apple. Then some watermelon can be added (athletes need to replace a great deal of fluid lost during exercise and watermelons provide it), along with grapefruit (for muscle repair), cranberries, cherries, oranges, pineapple (against sciatica, which athletes sometimes suffer), a bit of lemon, and cantaloupe.

I recommend alternating apple-based juices with carrot-based juices, since carrots provide quite a bit of needed fluid, yield a good supply of vitamins and minerals, and can be consumed pretty much like apple juice, mixing well with fruits.

For active individuals, I suggest a larger serving, both because these people burn up more calories and because the recommended apples, watermelon, and cantaloupe provide quite a bit of water—between 16 and 24 ounces either immediately after exercise (to replace the vitamins, minerals, and trace minerals that athletes use up, especially in hot weather) or midway through the afternoon to sustain energy.

Best Juice Recipes for Active People

. . . .

Cool Head Luke (page 117)

Energybomb (page 127)

Strawberry Surprise (page 131)

The Beet Goes On (page 136)

Potato Milk (page 146)

3

Total Juicing to Help Prevent Disease

We've all heard about the benefits of a low-fat, high-fiber diet and its effects on heart disease, cancer, diabetes, and other conditions caused by aging and overweight. The positive aspects of adopting this kind of diet are too many to be enumerated here, and are not the subject of this book. I would, however, like to talk about the fiber enrichment offered by home juicing and pulping.

Lower Cholesterol with Fresh Pulp
from Your Juicer

Fiber is the material that makes up the cell walls of plants. It helps plants take shape and perform their functions. There are many kinds of fiber in plants, and each type has distinct properties and specific uses.

Fiber has no caloric content. The fiber that passes through our digestive systems helps other foods pass through more efficiently, thereby preventing constipation.

Since all dietary fiber is not alike, we need to regularly eat and drink a variety of natural foods that contain a mixture of fiber types—and the fresher the better. The primary sources of fiber are whole grains, fresh fruits, and fresh vegetables.

When you juice fresh fruits or vegetables in the modern centrifugal juicers that separate the juice and the pulp, you get juices from one side of the machine and pulp from the other.

For providing vitamins and minerals, the juice is extremely important. But the fiber juicing produces as a by-product is equally important, which is why I have included in this book a separate section (Part 2) of recipes making use of the pulp.

Most of the pulp you produce with your juicer is not waste, but can be saved for a variety of uses. Besides its own store of vitamins and minerals, the pulp contains tremendous amounts of every type of essential fiber. It lends itself to making delicious foods, and some pulps can be used as fresh raw foods on their own.

For instance, in the juicer recipe section of this book (Part 2) you'll find directions to run carrots through your juicer first and then save the pulp for carrot cake, carrot salads, soups etc. When you juice tomatoes, the pulp can become the base for spaghetti sauce or homemade salsas. When you juice apples, the pulp can be served as apple-sauce—or as a topping for hot oat-bran cereal (another good source of fiber) or whole-grain pancakes or as a spread for toast. The pulp from most of the fruits you juice can be used for fresh dessert toppings and as the base for a number of whole-grain breads.

By using the juice from one side of your machine and the pulp from the other, you double your savings on the fresh fruits and vegetables you buy and double the benefits to your health.

Used regularly, fresh fruit and vegetable juices will help you lower your cholesterol, while the pulp will fulfill your daily fiber needs in a tasty alternative to "taking your medicine."

Best Recipes for Lowering Cholesterol with Pulp

Blender Soup (page 184)

Tomato Stuffed with Broccoli (page 188)

Potato-Apple Pancakes (page 202)

Stuffed Bell Peppers (page 206)

Chicken with Red Pepper Pulp (page 212)

Help for the Sensitive Stomach

Would it surprise anyone to learn that one of the three top-selling prescription medicines today is Tagamet, which is used to treat the stomach? On the whole we're unkind to our stomachs, and it's no wonder that on occasion they go on strike. The signals of protest the stomach sends can vary from gas and belching to a burning sensation and sometimes an intense upset.

Consider that all day long we pour very hot and very cold abrasive liquids down into our stomach—hot coffee and cold soft drinks. Then we eat fatty, hard-to-digest lunches, and we eat them too fast so that the stomach is overworked or we go for long periods without putting anything into our stomachs to absorb the naturally occurring stomach acids, formed to process food that never comes.

The fact is that stomach ulcers and other such conditions are some of our most common ailments. But fresh juices can do wonders for ulcers and can help your stomach not only survive but thrive.

Just What Is an Ulcer?

Simply put, an ulcer is an erosion of the stomach wall or the first segment of the duodenum (the first part of the small intestine) caused by stomach acids. The stomach is usually able to protect itself against these acids, but this protection can be erased by bacterial infection, which breaks down the wall's protective lining, or by certain things we eat, drink, or take as medicine that break down the wall, including alcohol, aspirin, ibuprofen, indomethacin, and steroids. The erosion can also be aggravated by smoking.

If you suspect that you have an ulcer, the first step is to go to your doctor to be tested to make certain it is not merely indigestion.

If you do have an ulcer, here are some things you can do to help alleviate the problem:

- If you smoke, stop. Besides helping your stomach, this will improve every other aspect of your life.
- If you drink coffee (caffeinated or decaf), stop. The coffee stimulates the release of gastric juices.
- If you drink alcohol, cut back. Like coffee, alcohol stimulates the production of gastric juices.
- Restrict your intake of salt. The same way salt can eat into ice on sidewalks and can eat through the fender of a car, it can exacerbate an ulcer.
- Cut out aspirin and aspirin-like products and don't use steroids.
- Use polyunsaturated vegetable oil; the linoleic acid it contains counters the bad effects of aspirin and other ulcer-inducing substances.
- Drink fresh vegetable juice every day.

Most people agree that green cabbage juice is the most helpful juice for ulcers. A quart of cabbage juice, consumed throughout the day, seems to be the ideal amount to help an ulcer problem.

A friend of mine, a corporate executive, had a serious ulcer some years ago. She went to a doctor for the problem, but the treatment didn't seem to work; she didn't get any better. Her husband recommended that she try cabbage-juice therapy. Her doctor was outraged at this and told her her condition would worsen and that he did not want to be responsible. Nevertheless, she drank a quart of cabbage juice in four installments each day for two weeks, while holding her nose. The juice had to be prepared fresh each time. Not only did the pain go away, it's never come back. That was ten years ago.

This story is true, but the solution may not work for

everyone. It is important in dealing with ulcers to consult a doctor first. In addition, you may wish to consult a doctor of nutrition.

Space the juice over the whole day, drinking small servings (4 to 6 ounces) at regular intervals, and eat something (preferably bland) with the juice. You don't want to drink the juice by itself; it could overstimulate the gastric juices when the stomach has too little to work on. You can eat a breadstick or salt-free cracker with each glass of cabbage juice.

If you find that you dislike the flavor of cabbage juice, you can modify the taste by adding carrot juice. It is my favorite all-around vegetable juice and is also very good by itself for ulcers. The carrot juice will help sweeten the cabbage juice, and will give you a one-two punch against the ulcer.

You can, of course, reverse the proportion of the juice and add another vegetable or two to make it tastier; use mostly carrots with a nearly equal proportion of fresh green cabbage and then add a bit of any other vegetable to adjust the taste to your liking. (See the recipe for Tummy Salad, which uses the four Cs: carrots, cabbage, celery— and cherries.)

When using cabbage in a juice, especially as a weapon against stomach ulcers, make only enough at one time for two or three hours, since, as I mentioned earlier, cabbage juice is fairly powerful stuff and develops a disagreeable odor if left too long in liquid form. Make sure to refrigerate the juice you are going to use later from your current batch. And don't ever add salt to change the flavor, since the salt tends to aggravate the ulcer.

Top Stomach Solutions

· ·

Carrot Prime (page 101)

V-6 Power Lunch (page 115)

Tummy Salad (page 119)

The Kitchen Sink (page 142)

Fizzy Georgia (page 161)

The Battle Against Cancer

Everyone who reads newspapers knows that a multitude of things in our modern world dramatically increase the risk of contracting cancer: tobacco products and asbestos, radiation and fatty foods, exposure to the sun and constipation. The results of cancer studies are released almost weekly. Researchers find enticing clues indicating that if not yet curable, cancer is at least predictable and to some extent preventable under certain circumstances.

One famous study by William Haenszel, Ph.D., found that Japanese who moved to the United States lowered their incidence of stomach cancers, which are fairly common in Japan. There was a trade-off, however: once in the United States, they developed more cancer of the breast, colon, uterus, prostate, and ovaries. Their cancer profile gradually became very much as ours has traditionally been, suggesting that environment and lifestyle have more to do with contracting certain kinds of cancer than does heredity.

Dr. Haenszel and fellow researchers took their work one step further and looked at the way diet affects the incidence of cancer. Dr. Haenszel began keeping statistics on people in similar socioeconomic and age groups who had colon cancer compared with those who did not. When he conducted extensive interviews about eating habits, an interesting piece of information emerged: those in the study group who were free of colon cancer reported eating a great deal more cabbage than those who had colon cancer.

The Dietary Link

This and similar findings prompted researchers to spend more and more time concentrating not only on the link between cancer and certain foods, but also *on the connection between those who did not have cancer and the kinds of foods they ate.*

Early in 1992 big headlines appeared in newspapers across the country announcing that broccoli was an excellent weapon for holding off cancer. Researchers at Johns Hopkins University School of Medicine isolated a substance in broccoli that promotes the production of enzymes in the body's cells to guard against tumors. Over the years, scientists have found both natural and synthetic compounds that incite this reaction by the body's own cells, but nothing does it so well—or so naturally— as the sulforaphane abundant in broccoli and other cruciferous vegetables, such as brussels sprouts and cauliflower. The importance of the 1992 news is that the study quoted found a *significantly* reduced risk of cancer in those who regularly ate cruciferous vegetables compared with those who did not.

Although the Johns Hopkins study made headlines, it merely added to what scientists already knew. What follows is a set of recommendations for decreasing the risk of cancer issued by the National Cancer Institute way back in 1985:

1. Increase your fiber intake to a total of 25 to 35 grams per day.
2. Lower your fat intake to 30 percent of daily calories.
3. *Eat more cruciferous vegetables,* such as brussels sprouts, cabbage, broccoli, cauliflower, rutabagas, and turnips.
4. Eat foods high in vitamins A and C.
5. Reduce your exposure to aflatoxins, which are naturally occurring molds that can grow on improperly stored nuts, grains, and seeds and are potent carcinogens (cancer-causers).
6. If you drink alcohol, drink only in moderation (two or fewer drinks a day), especially if you smoke, which greatly increases the negative effects of alcohol.
7. Whenever possible, bake, oven-broil, or microwave meats instead of barbecuing or frying at high temperatures. This reduces the formation of potentially carcinogenic substances.

The Beta-Carotene Connection

Beta-carotene is naturally occurring vitamin A, which has been shown in numerous studies to be important in maintaining the body's resistance to stress, the common cold, various infections, and disorders of the skin. A vitamin A deficiency can make you vulnerable to colds, and once you get a cold, you lose even more vitamin A—a vicious downward spiral.

More significant for our discussion of cancer, however, is the fact that a lack of vitamin A has been shown to undermine the ability of the body's tissues to repair themselves, which results in a susceptibility to lung problems (especially emphysema), infections, and cancer.

A Norwegian study released in 1975 paid special attention to the smoking and eating habits of 8,278 typical males in that country. The study concluded that those whose diets had insufficient vitamin A had a significantly higher incidence of cancer.

In this country, an important 1989 study was conducted at Rush–Presbyterian–St. Luke's Medical Center in Chicago. Richard Shekelle and his team studied two groups of 500 men, one group with high-carotene diets, the other with low-carotene diets. The high-carotene diet group developed only two incidences of lung cancer, while the low-carotene group developed fourteen over a period of nineteen years. Put another way, a cross-section of Americans are seven times more likely to develop lung cancer on a low-carotene diet than on a high-carotene diet.

The best natural source of beta-carotene is none other than the carrot. "But how many carrots can I eat in a day?" you might ask. That's where juicing comes in. If you consume two raw carrots a day, your protection against certain types of cancer will be improved many times. And you can easily *drink* those two carrots either alone or with other fresh vegetables in a tasty juice.

The nice thing about the beta-carotene group is that it is not limited to carrots (although you can hide carrots in plenty of other juicing recipes), so you can use a variety of carotene-rich natural foods in your regular diet and in your juicing. And you can make delicious juices by sticking strictly to the beta-carotene group.

The Beta-Carotene Group

apricots
asparagus
broccoli
carrots
dark leaf lettuce
mangoes
papayas
pumpkins
sweet potatoes
winter squash

Think of the beta-carotene group as an insurance policy against cancer.

Calcium: The Overlooked Cancer Fighter?

In several epidemiological studies reported within the last few years, scientists have found surprising new links between various nutrients and a lowered incidence of certain types of cancer.

One of the most surprising was the link between a good supply of calcium in the diet and in the body, and a low incidence of certain cancers. We have always associated calcium with strong bones and teeth, but now it seems calcium may also play a role in protecting us against cancer, especially cancer of the colon.

Calcium, we know, comes from dairy products, but a significant number of people cannot properly digest dairy products. Vegetables also provide substantial calcium.

High-Calcium Vegetables

beet greens
broccoli
collard greens
kale
kohlrabi
mustard greens
okra
turnip greens

An important connection also exists between vitamin D and calcium. Vitamin D, which is produced by the body when it is exposed to sunlight, helps the body to properly absorb calcium from food.

If the sun is out, put on a hat and apply sunscreen, and make yourself a glass of fresh juice that contains one or more of the calcium-rich vegetables listed above. Go outside and sip it while working in the garden, sitting in the park, or taking your daily walk. The sun will trigger your body's production of vitamin D, which in turn will help you absorb the calcium you're putting into your body by drinking your juice.

The Top Five Cancer Fighters

Carrots. Carrots are high in beta-carotene; when juiced they are extremely sweet; they are inexpensive; they stay relatively fresh for a fair amount of time; you can raise them easily in your own garden if you want to; and you can make a variety of delicious fresh juices using carrot juice as your starting point.

Broccoli. Because it belongs to the cabbage family, broccoli gets high marks in heading off cancer; it contains plenty of beta-carotene and is very high in calcium. Juice it, eat it in salads, steam it as a side dish.

Lettuce. When you go for lettuce to use in your juices (and lettuce is a terrific way to get plenty of natural water into your diet), remember that the darker the leaf, the more nutrition. (Iceberg lettuce is the least nutritious of all.) Lettuce can help prevent cancer, and is also a wonderful source of vitamin C.

Cabbage. As I said earlier, cabbage is good for sensitive stomachs, and it's also excellent as a cancer preventive. It is low in fat and extremely low in sodium. Use green cabbage for juicing, as it is tastier than red cabbage. Drink it as soon as possible after juicing, before it takes on a strong odor. And don't forget brussels sprouts, a member of the cabbage family. They are excellent for helping in the fight against cancer. I like to use brussels sprouts as an addition to carrot juice.

Turnips. The turnip is one of those vegetables that people either love or hate. A member of the cabbage family, the lowly turnip is a favorite among cancer-prevention experts. If it has one drawback, it is that it is high in sodium. If you're on a low-sodium diet, avoid turnips. If you're not, turnips—and especially turnip greens—are excellent for juicing. Turnips and greens contain large amounts of calcium, magnesium, and potassium. When you juice turnips, however, you'll want to use other vegetables to improve the taste. I find that fresh spinach and carrots help quite a bit, and brings its own arsenal of good nutrients. Other similarly valuable greens are collards and kale.

A Word on Fiber

Fiber is one of the best things you can eat on a daily basis to avoid cancer. As I said earlier, fiber performs a variety of bodily cleansing actions, especially helping to establish regularity. The pulp from your juicing is rich in cancer-preventing fiber.

Top Anti-Cancer Juice and Pulp Recipes

. . . .

Broccoli Blast (page 105)

Carrot Fruit Juice (page 109)

Apri-Cran Juice (page 110)

Broccoli Bush (page 116)

Simple Soup (page 184)

4

Essential Ingredients

Probably no one would argue that organically grown produce is better for us than produce that is sprayed with chemicals, picked unripe, and artificially stimulated to reach a pseudo-ripeness on its arrival at the local market. Yet few of us go to the trouble to search out organically grown produce. It is more expensive, less convenient, and often *looks* flawed to our eye.

. If you conduct an experiment and buy, let's say, a Golden Delicious apple from the produce section of the supermarket and a Golden Delicious apple from the local organic-food store, you will see some obvious differences. Have a friend or family member help you with this experiment. Blindfold yourself and have your partner hold each of the apples under your nose. See if you can pick out the organically grown apple by smell. Remember that your sense of smell is ten thousand times stronger than your sense of taste. Without your sense of smell, most things taste pretty much the same.

Which of the apples calls up a distinct image of an apple orchard in late summer, the branches straining under the burden of ripened fruit? Which apple makes you think of fake display fruit?

The *originality* of the fruits and vegetables you use in your juicing dictates the effectiveness of the juicing in promoting your overall health. I use the word "originality" here to mean the origin of the fruit or vegetable—its pedigree, its authenticity. The fresher the fruits or vegetables, the richer they are in vitamins, minerals, and other essential nutrients. The freer they are of chemicals and other enhancers, the more nutritious they are. The closer the fruits and vegetables are to their origin in the earth, the more delicious your juices will be.

There is really no comparison between those two apples.

Some of us are spoiled, of course, because we live in areas where stores selling organically grown produce are fairly common, while others live in parts of the country where you'd need a bounty hunter to help you find an organic-food store. Fortunately, even the larger chains of supermarkets are listening to their customers these days. Several of the national chains now have organic-produce sections in their stores, and many independently owned grocery stores are also adding or expanding organic-food sections.

The Next Best Thing

Although there is a gulf between the purity and quality of organically grown fruits and vegetables and chemically protected produce, any produce section still offers you a better juice option than bottled and canned fruit and vegetable juices.

Those perfect-looking apples are usually picked before they are tree-ripened and are treated and then transported hundreds of miles in a truck. But in many instances, they are a week or less removed from the tree. Take a walk through the aisle that features canned and bottled juices. How long removed from the tree do you think the apples that produced that juice are? Bend down and peer back through the rows of apple juice. See the bottle way in the back? How long do you think that bottle will sit on the shelf even after the bottle out front is sold? Two weeks? A month? Two months?

When you've pushed your cart back to the fresh produce aisles, fill it with carrots and lettuce and apples. While you're checking out, besides considering how much fresher the juice you are about to make will be, consider how much more economical it will be. You can make about 8 ounces of fresh apple juice from a pound of apples. If the apples cost you forty-nine cents a pound, that's forty-nine cents for a nice, fresh glass of apple juice brimming with vitamins and minerals. If you buy the bagged apples, they usually are cheaper per pound. And you can make good use of the pulp that comes as a by-product of your juicing.

Don't overlook the fact that you have a tremendous resource person at the produce department of your local supermarket. Most of the people who work in produce know exactly where each of their products comes from. Don't be afraid to ask the produce person on duty which of the produce is freshest, which comes from your own state or even from this country. Although some of the produce may have been shipped from as far away as

South America, some is only a few days removed from its source. Your greengrocer can be a tremendous help in ensuring that your juices are as fresh as you can possibly make them.

On the Road to Health

Almost every part of this country enjoys a wonderful annual tradition: the roadside fruit and vegetable stand.

When a region's fruits and vegetables are in season, those stands open to sell the products sometimes merely hours removed from the field or orchard. Some even invite you to pick your own, the ultimate in freshness.

When the season in your area arrives, make a day of it. Come up with a Saturday or Sunday route that will take you through all the nearby farming areas so that you can load up on the freshest of the local fruits and vegetables. Turn it into an adventure.

Just as you've done with the greengrocer at your supermarket, strike up a conversation with the farmers who man the roadside stands. Ask where you can buy fresh fruits and vegetables at other times of the year. Some of these farmers man their stands for only a few months, but often their harvest season extends months before and after. They also can often tell you who might have a small orchard of "antique" apple trees and might welcome people coming by to pick their own apples for a few dollars. Some of the most delicious apple juices I've ever made came from "antique" apples, those species that have been in this country for hundreds of years but today are little known and cultivated by only a handful of dedicated farmers.

Do It Yourself

If juice from store-bought produce is better than canned or bottled juice, and organic produce is better than chemically treated produce, and untreated produce from a local farmer's roadside stand is better still, what is the best, most satisfying source of fresh fruits and vegetables?

You are.

There is absolutely, positively nothing better than walking into your own garden to pick your own fresh fruits and vegetables and turning them into fresh juice a few minutes later.

We plant fruits and vegetables each year and enjoy nothing more than having friends over and sharing fresh juice with them that has just come from the garden.

Even city-dwellers can make the best of urban garden plots, and suburbanites are well placed to set a patch aside out back. Botanists at agriculturally oriented colleges have come up with many dwarf species that flourish in small plots of land. Inner-city gardeners grow dwarf apple trees in spaces no bigger than a dining-room table—and enjoy their harvest by bringing their ripe apples from the tree to the juicer.

In a world that is too often overwhelmingly stressful, psychologists have begun urging people to take up quiet, relaxing hobbies, and gardening is high on the list. One delight of gardening, of course, is that you can directly benefit from the fruits—and vegetables—of your labors.

A Gold Mine in a Glass

It's difficult to discuss the varied benefits of fresh fruit and vegetable juices without sounding like an evangelist. But to speak about them with any less enthusiasm would be to fail to represent their far-reaching effects.

There's only one way to say it: regularly drinking fresh fruit and vegetable juice to supplement your balanced diet is a means of assuring yourself that you have done everything good that you can do for yourself from a dietary standpoint. You have provided an arsenal of vitamins, minerals, and trace elements with which your body can repair itself, meet its metabolic needs, and fight off sickness. And you've done it in a quick, efficient, and pleasant way.

You've taken a giant step toward lengthening your life and improving its quality.

Flushing vs. Fueling

Some discussions of juicing promote the idea that fruit juices are used to flush toxins from our bodies, while vegetable juices serve to fuel and build our bodies. In discussions of fresh juices, you may see fruit juices referred to as "cleansers" and vegetable juices as "buffers" (that help lessen shocks to the system) or "builders."

This is an oversimplification. Tomato and pineapple juices, for instance, perform both cleansing *and* buffering duties.

In the following section you'll find a thorough guide to fresh fruit and vegetable juices. For each fruit or vegetable, I discuss how and how not to juice it, what vitamins and minerals and other important substances it contains, and exactly what it does for the body.

Fruit Juices

The listings of vitamins and minerals under the heading "Good source of" are based on fruits or vegetables containing 8 percent or more of the Recommended Daily Allowance of that vitamin or mineral. Folate and pantothenic acid are part of the B group of vitamins but currently have no numerical listing in that group. Under the heading "Good for," the areas of health that specific juices impact is based on currently available scientific research.

Apple

Just as the carrot is the staple in juicing vegetables, the apple is the staple in juicing fruits. The apple yields a great deal of raw juice, and the pectin it contains efficiently removes toxins and promotes regularity. The harder varieties of apples make juice with a pleasanter consistency. Don't be concerned by the cloudiness of your apple juice; it's quite natural. Store-bought apple juice has been filtered.

When juicing store-bought apples, wash them thoroughly to remove any residues of chemicals with which they may have been sprayed. Use apple juice as your basic fruit juice, adding other fruits to alter the flavor and the consistency. Or use apple juice to thin out fruit juices which are thick and intensely flavored, such as prune or strawberry. Apples can be juiced without removing the skin or seeds.

Pulp: Save for a variety of uses, from applesauce and topping for pancakes to the basis for cakes and muffins.

Good source of: Vitamin C.

Combines well with: This is the universal fruit mixer; can be mixed with any fruit.

Good for: Healthy skin and hair. High vitamin C content protects against colds and flu. Pectin cleans out toxins and helps maintain regularity. Eases indigestion. Good juice for a weight-loss program. Flushes kidneys and liver. Good for the heart: no saturated fat or cholesterol.

Apricot

The apricot is the fruit world's beta-carotene champion. The little fruit is loaded with the cancer-preventing substance—and is delicious besides. For juicing, pick apricots that are firm and not overly ripe; remove the pit first.

Pulp: Can be used in a variety of ways, especially as a puree, as an ingredient in preserves, or as a dessert topping.

Good source of: Beta-carotene; potassium; vitamin A, C, E, K.

Combines well with: Berry, apple.

Good for: Helping prevent cancer of the lung, stomach, bladder, esophagus, and throat, treating colds and flu.

Berry
(boysenberries, raspberries, blueberries, blackberries, currants, etc.)

Berries make a wonderful summertime treat when turned into juice. They are filled with potassium, a mineral which we often lack, since our too-salty diet robs the body of it. Berry juices are intense and should be cut with either apple juice or spring water (further lowering their already low fat content). A cup of unjuiced blackberries has only 74 calories, while a cup of raspberries has only 60! Try using berries to flavor watermelon juice.

Pulp: Like berry juice, berry pulp is strongly flavored and can be used for a variety of purposes, from purees to toppings for desserts and whole-grain waffles or pancakes.

Good source of: Vitamin C, folate, magnesium, and potassium.

Combines well with: Apple, other berry, pineapple.

Good for: Regulating blood pressure by providing potassium to balance sodium in the diet. Appetite stimulant. Digestive aid. Has laxative properties. A tool for weight loss when cut with apple juice or water.

(For strawberry, see separate listing.)

Cherry

The juice of cherries is powerfully flavored and should be cut with water or lighter juices such as apple, or used to enliven more basic juices. Cherries must be pitted before juicing. Discard those that are too ripe or not ripe enough; fruit should be firm and glowing. Since cherries come in a variety of types, from sweet to sour, you'll want to consider what additional fruit or vegetable juice you can use to complement the particular cherry's taste.

Pulp: Save for use as a dessert topping, for making jam, or for additional uses, such as sorbet.

Good source of: Vitamin C; potassium.

Combines well with: Apple, melon, water.

Good for: Reducing acid in the bloodstream. When cut with apple juice or spring water, a good tool for weight loss. Eases indigestion and constipation. Can be used to treat anemia and gout.

Cranberry

Most people can't get fresh cranberries past their lips without adding some sweeter flavors, since cranberries are highly acidic. The health benefits of cranberries are so great, however, that it's worth the effort to put more cranberries into your diet. Cranberries can be mellowed with any of the blander fruit juices, such as apple or melon, and can also liven up some of the basic vegetable juices, such as carrot. Cranberries should be very thoroughly washed before juicing, and the fresher you can get them the better, although they travel fairly well.

Pulp: An excellent addition to muffins, healthful cakes, and whole-grain breads.

Good source of: Vitamin C. Also contains quinic acid, a diuretic.

Combines well with: Apple, watermelon, pear.

Good for: Cleansing a variety of organs of infections and toxins, especially the urinary tract, the kidneys, and liver, while improving digestion and curing some skin problems, such as acne.

Grape

The grape has been used as a source of fresh juice for all of recorded history. For the modern juicer, the beauty is that grapes can be processed with skin, seeds, and stems. The juice of most grapes is healthfully drunk just by itself, although some varieties that are on the sour side benefit from mixing with apple or melon juices. Fresh grape juice will be cloudy, much like apple juice; clear bottled grape juice has been filtered, losing many nutrients.

Pulp: Can be used as compost, as fertilizer for gardens, and as feed for songbirds.

Good source of: Vitamin B1, C, and E; potassium.

Combines well with: Apple, water, melon, peach.

Good for: Cleaning the kidneys and liver. Useful in a weight-loss program. Improves digestion, helping to prevent constipation. A guard against certain cancers.

Grapefruit

Let me repeat my caution about juicing citrus fruit (grapefruits, oranges, tangerines, lemons, limes, etc.): Citrus juices should not be drunk every day, especially if your metabolism is not high, as it is when you are young or extremely physically active. The body has difficulty metabolizing citrus acids, and drinking an excessive amount of citrus juices can actually undermine calcium buildup in the bones and teeth. When juicing any citrus fruit, remove the skin and discard it; also remove as many seeds as possible, but leave as much of the white pith as you can, as this is the depository of many nutrients. Then quarter the fruit and process it.

Pulp: Can be used as compost, or in jams and jellies.

Good source of: Vitamin C.

Combines well with: Apple, strawberry.

Good for: Heading off colds and flus. Also effective for weight loss. Speeds the healing of minor bruises, due to the cooperation of bioflavonoids and vitamin C in increasing the effectiveness of the capillaries in speeding re-pairing elements to a bruise and removing damaged cells. This same benefit to the capillaries is especially good for pregnant women.

Lemon

Like grapefruit juice, lemon juice should be used spar-ingly: no more than three times a week if you are seden-tary. The best way to drink freshly processed lemon juice is to dilute it heavily with spring water. As with grape-fruit, remove the skin and discard it; remove as many seeds as you can; leave on as much of the white pith as possible; quarter the lemon and process it. Use lemon juice to add flavor to apple or melon juices or to help pre-serve the freshness of other juices.

Pulp: Discard or use as compost.

Good source of: Vitamin C.

Combines well with: Water, potato, apple, pear, strawberry.

Good for: As with grapefruit, lemons are good for treating minor bruises, for pregnant women, as a tool for weight loss, and, of course, to prevent or treat colds and flu.

Lime

Lime juice has many similarities to lemon juice, but it is lower in acid and therefore does not need as much cutting with water or other fruit juices. As with the other citrus fruits, peel first, remove the seeds, and juice the fruit and the white pith.

Pulp: Discard or use as compost.

Good source of: Vitamin C.

Combines well with: Apple, strawberry.

Good for: Colds and flu, indigestion and skin problems, liver problems, constipation, anemia and other blood problems.

Melon

All melons have a high water content, and are therefore excellent for keeping the urinary tract active and healthy, for keeping the body supplied with fluids, and for flushing the kidneys. Most of the water is in the meat of the melon, while the largest concentration of nutrients is in the rind and skin. Scrape off the outer skin, and scoop out the seeds and discard them so as not to damage your juicer. Juice the rind and the meat. Although each melon has a flavor all its own, none of the juices is very strong, so it is often preferable to jazz it up with another, more concentrated juice. Try berry or cherry juice.

Pulp: Can be frozen and served as a fiber-rich sorbet, a cooling treat on a hot day—especially topped with berry or other fruit puree saved from previous juicing.

Good source of: Vitamins A, C, folate; potassium.

Combines well with: Cherry, cranberry.

Good for: Flushing and cleansing the body, especially the urinary tract. Promotes regularity. Good for the skin. (For watermelon, see separate listing.)

Orange

As I said earlier, the body needs to metabolize citric acid in order to prevent the leaching of calcium from the bones and teeth. Therefore, if your metabolism has slowed because of aging, ill health, or sedentary habits, go easy on orange juice—no more than three glasses a week. If you're young or extremely active, orange juice will not have a deleterious effect; I recommend 8 to 12 ounces a day. There is no comparison between the fresh juice you make for yourself and the kind you buy at the store. The store-bought orange juice has been pasteurized, destroying the essential enzymes. As with other citrus fruits, peel the skin, remove the seeds, and juice the meat and the white pith.

Pulp: Discard.

Good source of: Vitamin C, B1, folate; potassium.

Combines well with: Apple, papaya, strawberry.

Good for: Colds and flu. Can be used effectively in weight-loss programs, especially if slightly cut with water. Aids digestion, and clears up some skin problems.

Peach

Besides bursting with flavor, a ripe, firm peach also bursts with vitamins and minerals. To juice peaches, wash them, slice them into pieces that your juicer can accommodate, and discard the pits. Peach juice is thick and rich and is best diluted with other fruit juices, especially if you are juicing for weight loss.

Pulp: Can be used for a dessert or pancake topping or can be mixed with peach preserves to thicken and add taste.

Good source of: Vitamin C; potassium.

Combines well with: Apple, grape, water.

Good for: Cleansing bowels, especially breaking up constipation. Improves digestion. Oxygenates blood.

Pear

Pears are one of the juiciest fruits. Ripe pears produce a thick, rich, flavorful drink that can be used as is or be diluted with water or other juices such as apple or grape. For juicing, merely wash, pull out the stem, and cut to fit your juicer.

Pulp: Can be used to enrich jams and preserves or as a very sweet fruit topping or compote.

Combines well with: Apple, lemon, water.

Good for: Cleansing the urinary and gastrointestinal tracts—one of the best cleansers, in fact. Great cure for constipation. Enlivens the liver.

Pineapple

I love to go to the produce section and pick through the pineapples, sniffing out the ripe ones to take home. A really ripe pineapple has a strong, enticing aroma. Once you get the pineapple home, lay it on its side on a cutting board and chop off both ends. Then stand the pineapple on end and cut off the rough skin. Cut the meat into long spears and juice. Fresh pineapple juice will go a long way if you cut it with an equal amount of water. Serve it over ice.

Pulp: Use as a dessert topping or as the main ingredient in pineapple upside-down cake.

Good source of: Vitamin B1, C; manganese. (If I feel a cold or flu coming on, I much prefer pineapple to citrus for my vitamin C.) The enzyme bromelin helps stabilize the acid-alkaline balance of body fluids.

Combines well with: Apple, berry.

Good for: Colds and flu. Excellent weight-loss tool. Improves digestion.

Prune

To get the best juice from prunes, you need to soak them overnight in hot water. Since this takes more time, I usually prepare quite a bit at once: a dozen large prunes can be soaked in a quart of hot water. Make certain the prunes are pitted—you don't want to damage your juicer. Keep the water in which the prunes were soaked. Juice the prunes and then use a blender to mix in the soaking water. If the mixture is still too thick, dilute it with more water.

Pulp: Use as a topping for whole-grain waffles or in muffins.

Good source of: Vitamin B6; copper, potassium. The laxative action of prunes is well known; it comes from two acids: benzoic and quinic.

Combines well with: Apple, water.

Good for: Easing constipation. Can also be used in a weight-loss program.

Strawberry

The strawberry is another fruit that makes a rich, thick juice that lends itself to being cut with apple juice or water. To juice, merely wash the fruit and remove the stems. (You'll want to thoroughly wash commercially grown strawberries, because they are frequently treated with chemicals.)

Pulp: Can be used as a topping for waffles and pancakes or for desserts.

Good source of: Vitamin C, K; manganese, and potassium.

Combines well with: Other berry, water, apple, citrus.

Good for: You name it, strawberry juice is good for it: skin conditions; constipation; losing weight (diluted with water); and relieving gout, minor muscle discomfort from overexertion, and rheumatism.

Watermelon

Watermelon juice is a perfect source of the fluids your body needs daily. When juicing a watermelon, trim away the skin and remove the seeds but juice the rind and the meat. The resulting juice is more bland than just about any fruit juice you can make, the sugar content is relatively low, and it does not need to be diluted. In fact, watermelon juice (along with apple and grape juice) is perfect for diluting richer, thicker juices.

Pulp: Freeze and serve as a low-calorie sorbet.

Good source of: Vitamin B6, C.

Combines well with: Cherry, cranberry.

Good for: Cleansing various body systems, including the bladder, kidneys, and liver. Good as a weight-loss drink. Good for the skin. An aid for constipation.

Vegetable Juices

Artichoke, Globe or French

This interesting vegetable should be lightly parboiled before juicing in a nonreactive stainless-steel or glass pot (anything else causes the artichoke to discolor). Strip away the leaves until you reach the heart of the artichoke, which is tender and meaty. The leaves fit easily into your juicer; the heart must be sliced and inserted in pieces. Artichoke juice is an acquired taste and is best mixed with blander juices, such as celery.

Pulp: Can be used for soup.

Good source of: Vitamins C, K; magnesium, phosphorus.

Combines well with: White wine, carrot, cucumber, tomato.

Good for: Supplementing other sources of calcium for strong bones.

Artichoke, Jerusalem

No relation to the globe or French artichoke above, the Jerusalem artichoke resembles the potato. It grows as a tuber underground, with a blossom aboveground which looks like a small sunflower. Although Jerusalem artichokes have traditionally been used as livestock feed, they are quite suitable for human food. Like potato juice, though, Jerusalem artichoke juice tastes bland, and you'll want to mix in other juices to make it more palatable. The old standby, carrot juice, works well.

Pulp: Can be used to make a potato-like pancake.

Good source of: Vitamin B1; niacin, iron, phosphorus.

Combines well with: Parsnip, lemon, and carrot.

Good for: Diabetes and hypoglycemia. Also very good for a weight-loss program, reducing the craving for sweets.

Asparagus

Unfortunately, asparagus is too expensive to enjoy frequently; I recommend it occasionally to enhance other juices, especially carrot. Use the entire stalk when you juice it, but scrape off the tough, stringy outer skin of the lower half of the stalk.

Pulp: Can be mixed with avocado and made into a dip.

Good source of: Vitamin B1, B2, C, E, K, folate.

Combines well with: Carrot, celery, lettuce, tomato, sprouts, or beet greens.

Good for: Cleansing the kidneys. Contains properties that can guard against most types of cancer, since it contains carotene, vitamin C, and selenium. Good for reducing acidity in the blood and skin. Relieves gout. Helps treat rheumatism and neuritis.

Beet and Beet Greens

The beet is one of the most nutritious vegetables, and juiced along with the greens, the juice is terrific. It's strongly flavored, however, and mixing it liberally with carrots, celery, or lettuce juice (or all three) makes it more palatable. Since this juice is so strong, it is best to use it in small amounts only a few times a week at most. Too much beet juice can upset a sensitive stomach.

Pulp: Use for soups or mix with carrot pulp for salad topping.

Good source of: Vitamin C, K, folate; magnesium.

Combines well with: Carrot, cucumber, asparagus, apple, endive.

Good for: In moderation, beet-and-beet-green juice is good for a variety of problems, especially those involving the bladder, kidney, and liver. Helps improve red blood cells and build the efficiency of the circulatory system, and is therefore good for the heart, as well as effective for treating both high and low blood pressure. Also thought to be effective in preventing liver and gall bladder cancers, and a good tool for weight loss.

Brussels Sprouts

Members of the cabbage family, brussels sprouts have
many of the same beneficial qualities. The juice from
brussels sprouts is pretty potent stuff, and it should be
consumed immediately; after a few hours the juice takes
on a strong smell. You can make a very nice juice by mixing carrot juice with brussels sprout juice.

Pulp: Can be mixed into salads.

Good source of: Vitamin A, B1, B6, C, E, K, folate;
potassium.

Combines well with: Carrot, string bean.

Good for: Treating stomach ulcers. Effective against
constipation. A very good cleansing agent for the kidneys
and liver.

Cabbage

This is another juice that you need to drink while it is
fresh—if it sits for two hours or more it develops an un-
palatable taste. Cabbage juice can be cut with water or
with vegetable juices that are on the bland side. A caution: consumed in too large quantities, cabbage juice can
cause gas in the intestines.

Pulp: Can be used as an ingredient in carrot salad.

Good source of: Vitamin C, E, K, folate; potassium.

Combines well with: Carrot, celery, parsnip, turnip.

Good for: Easing constipation. Treatment for stomach ulcers. Good for skin and hair. Cleanses kidneys and
bladder. Can relieve colitis.

Carrot

I consider the carrot the benchmark of the vegetable kingdom when it comes to juicing. The carrot keeps well; it juices beautifully and becomes very sweet; the pulp can be used in a variety of ways; and the juice is filled with good things to help the body. I always add some celery juice to balance the extreme sweetness. I find carrot juice a very calming drink—it has such wide-ranging good effects on the body, among them a neutralizing of the stomach and digestive tract, that its good effects seem to spread throughout the body.

Pulp: Many, many good uses. See recipe section.

Good source of: Vitamin A, B1, B6, folate, C, and K; potassium, and a variety of important trace minerals.

Combines well with: The universal vegetable mixer; mixes well with any vegetable.

Good for: The eyes (yes, it's true). Very good treatment for stomach ulcers. Excellent for defending against cancer. Relieves skin conditions, including acne. Cleanses the bladder and liver. Promotes appetite, aids digestion. Also excellent for weight loss.

Celery

As I said above, I don't have carrot juice unless I mix in some celery juice. They just go together so well. Celery juice is good on its own, too.

Pulp: Use in soups and salsas.

Good source of: Vitamin A, B6, folate, C, K; potassium, calcium.

Combines well with: Especially good with carrot, but can be used with any vegetable to balance flavor.

Good for: Cleansing the kidneys and liver. Useful for weight loss. Helps maintain both acid-alkaline balance in the blood and calcium levels. An excellent mixer with other, stronger juices. Treatment for gout and ulcers.

Cucumber

No vegetable juice is a better summer refresher. Cucumbers have an extremely high water content, and contain a large amount of all-important potassium, which is excellent for maintaining healthy, youthful skin. (That's why some beauty parlors place cucumber slices over their clients' eyes.) The only shortcoming of the cucumber is that, like the apple, it often comes waxed, and you don't want to juice the wax. But when you remove the skin, you also remove most of the vitamin A. Of course, some people develop intestinal gas when they eat the skins. I recommend keeping the skin if this is not a problem for you. I love a tall glass of half cucumber juice and half spring water over ice on a hot day.

Pulp: Can be made into a cool, creamy, low-cal dip.

Good source of: Folate, C, K.

Combines well with: Especially good with carrot and celery; excellent for cutting the strong tastes of other vegetable juices.

Good for: Cleansing the kidneys. A weight-loss tool. Helps lower high blood pressure. Excellent for skin problems. Excellent daily source of fluid.

Endive (Escarole, Chicory)

This salad green is not used much in this country because of its distinct bitter taste. It's a taste that's well worth acquiring, however, because this unique vegetable has a long list of benefits. Most people prefer to mix endive juice with other juices.

Pulp: Use in vegetable soup, or compost.

Good source of: Vitamin A, folate, pantothenic acid, and C; potassium, manganese.

Combines well with: Sprout, beet green.

Good for: Cleansing the bladder, kidneys, and liver. Very good for skin problems. Effective against constipation. Helpful in weight-loss programs. Good for the eyes.

Garlic

Jack and I have always considered garlic nature's medicine. Although low in nutrients, garlic has extremely strong bactericidal properties. We eat garlic regularly on just about anything we can think of. I don't recommend that you take a few bulbs of garlic and juice it into a super-powerful tonic; instead, occasionally drop a clove of garlic into vegetable juice you're making, especially into a juice that is strong in its own right.

Pulp: Discard.

Good source of: Bacteria-killers. Vitamin B1, C; potassium, calcium, copper, iron, magnesium, phosphorus, selenium.

Combines well with: Water, carrot, cabbage, cucumber, celery.

Good for: Avoiding colds and flu. Helps relieve constipation. Clears mucus.

Greens (Collard, Kale, Turnip, etc.)

Greens, long a staple in the Deep South, are excellent sources of chlorophyll and calcium. We don't typically think of juicing greens, but they lend themselves quite well to the practice. Juiced greens taste similar to cabbage, so you might want to mix them with other juices (celery, for instance). If you have a digestive intolerance for milk products, this is an excellent way to get all the calcium you need for strong bones and teeth.

Pulp: Can be used for soups.

Good source of: Vitamin A, B1, B2, and C, calcium, chlorophyll, and numerous minerals, including iron, magnesium, and potassium.

Combines well with: Kohlrabi, asparagus.

Good for: The blood, anemia, eyes, hair, and skin problems. Strengthens bones and teeth. Good defense against stomach and liver cancers. Effective cleanser. Relieves stomach ulcers and liver problems.

Kohlrabi

I thought about putting this into the exotics chapter because it is not much used, but it is widely available and is very similar in some ways to the turnip and radish. Kohlrabi juice is strong and should be mixed with milder juices.

Pulp: Can be used as an ingredient in dips.

Good source of: Vitamin B6, C; potassium.

Combines well with: Sprout, greens, beet greens, cucumber, carrot.

Good for: Lung and sinus problems; effective in clearing the mucous membranes. Good for certain skin problems, especially eczema. Effective as a weight-loss tool when cut with other vegetable juices.

Lettuce

A vast variety of lettuces are available. A rule of thumb is that the darker the lettuce, the more nutritious it is. Among the most nutritious varieties are romaine, buttercrunch, and Bibb. (Iceberg is one of the least nutritious.) Generally inexpensive and an excellent source of fluid, lettuce also offers many other benefits. The darker lettuces, which are rich in a number of important minerals, can have a fairly pronounced taste, so are best cut with other juices, especially carrot.

Pulp: Discard.

Good source of: Vitamin A, B1, C, K, folate; manganese, potassium.

Combines well with: Spinach, sprout, parsnip.

Good for: Healthy skin and hair. An excellent cleanser, especially for the liver. Has a calming effect—especially iceberg lettuce, which contains a mild natural opiate. A good drink for promoting weight loss by moderating appetite. Energizes the muscles, brain, and nerves.

Onion

Onions come in a variety of species, including pearl, yellow, Spanish, white, and red onions, shallots, and chives. All of these (along with leeks, scallions, and garlic) are members of the lily family. Onions range from sweet (Bermuda onions, members of the white and red onion families) to strong (smaller yellow onions). As with garlic, onions are good for fighting bacteria, but contain plenty of vitamin C besides, so if a germ does manage to get by the bacteria-killers, the vitamin C continues the fight. As with garlic, use slices of onions to supplement vegetable juice you are already making, especially the stronger juices such as cabbage. You can also add onion to perk up carrot juice or some of the sweeter, milder juices. Use white, red, or Spanish onions, which are sweeter and therefore easier to drink.

Pulp: Discard, use in compost, or add to vegetable soup.

Good source of: Vitamin C, folate, and bacteria-fighters.

Combines well with: Water, carrot, cabbage, tomato, squash.

Good for: Heading off colds and flu and fighting them once they arrive.

Parsley

Ounce for ounce, there is no more nutritious herb you can eat than parsley, yet it is typically used as a garnish and thrown away. The wonderful thing about parsley is that you don't have to eat or drink much of it to benefit. Next time parsley turns up on your plate, save it to eat last—it gives your mouth a fresh taste and smell. Parsley juice is very strong, so it is best to mix one part to about ten parts of another less potent juice.

Pulp: Sprinkle on salads.

Good source of: Vitamin A, C, E, folate; niacin, calcium, iron, magnesium, potassium.

Combines well with: Carrot, celery, cucumber, turnip.

Good for: Cleansing the urinary tract and the blood. Treats conditions of the kidneys and liver. Helps prevent many cancers such as kidney, liver, urinary tract. Good for circulatory deficiencies. Good for general heart health. Can be used for weight loss. Good for the eyes.

Parsnip

Here's another borderline exotic vegetable. We're discussing parsnips here because they are fairly readily available throughout the country, though you may need to look extra carefully to find them in some produce departments. Like carrot juice, parsnip juice is sweet and needs to be cut with milder juices. It's a nutritious addition to any juice regimen. Use only cultivated parsnips, as wild parsnips contain several poisons.

Pulp: Can be used as an ingredient in salads and to flavor cole slaw.

Good source of: Vitamin C, E, K, folate, pantothenic acid; magnesium, phosphorus.

Combines well with: Cabbage, potato, squash, lettuce.

Good for: Skin conditions, especially acne. Can be used as treatment (as with their first cousin, carrots) for stomach ulcers. Also, like carrots, good for the eyes. Cleanses the liver and bladder.

Pepper, Sweet

Jack, who in his life has experimented with just about every fruit and vegetable you can think of to see whether it can help the human body, once tried to drink hot peppers that he'd juiced. I consider Jack a pretty tough guy, but he didn't see any sense in pursuing his hot-pepper drink any further. "It was like drinking fire," he said. But drinking juice from sweet peppers is an entirely different experience. Sweet peppers (either green or red; red peppers are merely older green peppers) are very high in vitamin C, and the ripe, red peppers are also high in vitamin A. Sweet-pepper juice mixes well with quite a few other vegetable juices.

Pulp: Can be used in salsa.

Good source of: Vitamin A, B6, C, E, folate; potassium.

Combines well with: Tomato, carrot, squash, turnip, radish.

Good for: Helping to lower high blood pressure; bestows general good health to the heart. Good for healthy skin and eyes.

Potato

It may sound silly to consider juicing potatoes, but they are excellent sources of complex carbohydrates, and since they are so mild when juiced, they're great for mixing with stronger juices, such as cabbage and radish. The lowly potato is also one of the great bargains in the supermarket. When you juice potatoes, scrub the skins and leave them on. Most of the nutrients are in or near the skin. Cut the potatoes into slices and feed them into the juicer.

Pulp: Can be used for potato pancakes.

Good source of: Carbohydrates, a variety of vitamins (B1, B6, C, K, pantothenic acid), potassium, copper, niacin, magnesium.

Combines well with: Parsnip, lemon, carrot, squash.

Good for: Skin problems, gout, ulcer, and gastritis. General body cleanser.

Radish

Radish juice is very potent and requires extensive cutting with less overpowering juices; it should be used sparingly and is best not drunk on an empty stomach, even when mixed with other juices. Nibble on some salt-free crackers or breadsticks before drinking this one. It is a wonderful cleanser, however. An additional benefit of the radish is that it stays fresh much longer than less dense vegetables do.

Pulp: Can be used to perk up a salad or dip.

Good source of: Vitamin C, folate; potassium.

Combines well with: Potato, kohlrabi, carrot, cucumber, sweet peppers. Good for enlivening blander juices.

Good for: Sinus problems, skin problems, and as a weight-loss tool.

Scallion

A scallion is a green onion. Like other members of the onion family, the scallion works wonders in the sinuses, lungs, and mucous membranes. But because of its strong aroma, it is best used sparingly and mixed with other, less potent vegetable juices. As with garlic, it is usually best to drop a scallion or two into a vegetable drink you are making.

Pulp: Can be used in salsas and spaghetti sauces.

Good source of: Vitamin A, B2, folate, pantothenic acid, C; potassium, calcium, iron.

Combines well with: Water, carrot, cabbage: a little gives a bite to any juice.

Good for: Helping to clear mucous membranes, the lungs, and sinuses. Assists in killing germs. Can help with asthma.

Spinach

This is one of the most complete all-around vegetable juices you can make, for both cleansing and building. Strong in chlorophyll, spinach has properties that can increase the efficiency of every organ in the human body, from the gall bladder to the intestinal tract. Spinach juice can be difficult for the body to metabolize, so use it sparingly and always mixed with other juices—unless you are young or very active. For the average person, I recommend a few ounces of spinach juice per week.

Pulp: Compost or discard.

Good source of: Vitamin A, B2, B6, folate, biotin, C, E, K; potassium, calcium, magnesium, iron, manganese.

Combines well with: Lettuce, carrot, tomato, turnip.

Good for: Cleansing the kidneys, liver, and digestive tract. Improves regularity. Helps prevent bladder cancer, and stomach ulcers. Fight infection. Helps lower high blood pressure and maintain acid-alkaline balance.

Sprouts (Alfalfa, Bean, Cabbage, Radish, etc.)

You can easily juice just about any vegetable sprout and enjoy a very effective cleansing agent. Sprouts are also excellent for their cleansing effect. They are especially high in various trace minerals, but are also very rich in vitamins, especially C. Alfalfa sprouts are considered the best, offering an incredible array of vitamins.

Pulp: Use for compost.

Good source of: Vitamin B2, folate, pantothenic acid, C; phosphours, magnesium, zinc.

Combines well with: Asparagus, endive, lettuce, turnip.

Good for: The kidneys, liver, thyroid gland, and diseases of the blood. Also good for the eyes.

String Bean

Surprisingly tasty, fresh string-bean juice is high in a number of minerals. String beans are exceptionally easy to juice, and the juice mixes well with carrot juice.

Pulp: Discard or use for compost.

Good source of: B vitamins, chlorophyll, magnesium, potassium, and a significant amount of vegetable protein.

Combines well with: brussels sprout.

Good for: Blood and skin disorders. Can help diabetes by assisting the body in producing insulin. A weight-loss tool.

Squash, Summer

Summer squashes (zucchini and yellow squash, for example) are not as nutrient-rich as winter squashes, but lend themselves to easy juicing. The juice is very versatile, mellowing any number of stronger vegetable juices.

Pulp: Can be used for zucchini bread, etc.

Good source of: Vitamin C, folate; magnesium and potassium.

Combines well with: Radish, parsnip, sweet pepper, onion.

Good for: Cleansing, especially the kidneys and bladder. Helps maintain acid-alkaline balance.

Squash, Winter

The winter squashes (butternut, Hubbard, and acorn) are high in three of the best cancer-fighting substances found in nature: vitamin C, fiber, and beta-carotene. Juicing removes the fiber, but by saving the pulp and using it in a variety of recipes, you can enjoy its tremendous benefits. Winter squash is very high in calcium, so it is important in the diets of older people and those prone to weak bones. Unfortunately, many winter squashes are so hard that they cannot be properly juiced by some machines. The harder squash can best be handled by cutting them into strips and feeding them into the juicer, or by lightly cooking them before juicing. Squash that is cooked, even lightly, tends to stick to the inside of the juicer.

Pulp: Save for baked goods.

Good source of: Vitamin A and C, folate; potassium.

Combines well with: Radish, parsnip, sweet pepper, onion.

Good for: Cancer prevention. Strong bones and teeth. Healthy heart.

Tomato

Tomatoes are among my favorite vegetables to juice. They are also a source of very usable pulp. And they provide a great example of how fresh vegetable juice is worlds apart from a processed juice. Canned tomato juice is thick and salty because it is cooked before canning and salt is added to preserve it and supposedly to improve the taste. Freshly processed juice made from vine-ripened tomatoes is refreshing, light, and velvety and leaves an aftertaste like a fine wine. We enjoy growing our own tomatoes; we pick an armful of fresh tomatoes, bring them inside, juice them, mix in a bit of celery juice and perhaps the juice of a few carrots, and drink it right down.

Pulp: Save for spaghetti sauce and other Italian sauces, and for salsas.

Good source of: Vitamin A and C, and potassium.

Combines well with: Asparagus, artichoke (globe), parsley, cabbage, spinach, sweet pepper, onion.

Good for: Alleviating problems of the bladder, gall bladder, liver, kidney, and skin. Also very good as a weight-loss tool.

Turnip

People either love turnips or hate them. But no matter where you stand, you've got to admit that the turnip is one potent vegetable. It mixes well with other vegetables—one turnip blends particularly well with a half dozen big, ripe, juicy tomatoes.

Pulp: Can be added to cole slaw.

Good source of: A variety of vitamins and minerals, especially Vitamin C.

Combines well with: Spinach, carrot, sprout, parsley, cabbage, sweet pepper, tomato.

Good for: Improving skin problems, especially acne. Cleanses the liver and kidneys. Helps prevent cancer and bladder infections. Helps the eyes, especially in the prevention and treatment of cataracts. Builds the blood and helps anemia. Good for a weight-loss program.

A Walk on the Wild Side

Eating should be an adventure, a continuing experiment. I enjoy the "standard" foods, certainly, but I also enjoy experimenting when I cook and juice.

If you want to be creative, you may need to look for little out-of-the-way markets that handle some of the more unusual produce. In almost every part of the country, there are enclaves of people who know where to find such fruits and vegetables. If you're uncertain as to where these exotics can be found, ask the produce manager of your local supermarket.

A wide variety of fruits and vegetables are grown specifically for the Asian restaurant trade, and some are excellent for juicing experiments, although they can be difficult to find unless you live in a neighborhood with a preponderance of Asian grocery stores. Booklets are available in many grocery stores to help you find your way through these highly exotic fruits and vegetables.

If you feel tentative, pick up one or two exotic vegetables and add a conservative amount to your next glass of carrot and celery juice. If you like it, add a little more next time until you reach a point where it is just exotic enough for your taste. To simplify this process, juice your base juice first, rinse your juicer, then juice your exotics and keep their juice in a separate glass. Add a little at a time, stirring the exotic juice in with your basic carrot juice until you find a mixture that tastes good to you. You may eventually reach a point where you feel confident enough to begin with the exotic juices and then use some carrot juice to mellow it.

It's not only OK to experiment and be creative in your juicing, it is a sure way to enhance the experience—and to enlarge the arsenal of healthful fruits and vegetables you have at your fingertips.

Belgian Endive

Belgian endive belongs to the chicory family and should not be confused with escarole and curly endive. Used primarily in fancy salads, Belgian endive tends to be on the expensive side. It looks very similar to what is left if you peel the leaves away from a head of lettuce until you are down to a tiny shrub about five inches tall and a bit more than an inch in diameter. When juiced, the liquid is quite dark and should be used immediately, as it does not store well.

Pulp: Discard.

Good source of: Vitamin A, C, folate, pantothenic acid; manganese, potassium.

Combines well with: Carrot.

Good for: Cleansing urinary tract. Fights colds and flu.

Daikon Radish

The daikon radish is one of the easiest, most convenient vegetables you can use because all you need to do is scrub it, cut it into strips, and juice it. The daikon radish is a long, white vegetable; it should be firm and the color of piano keys. Its juice is very light and mild and mixes well with other juices.

Pulp: Discard.

Good source of: Vitamin C, folate; potassium.

Combines well with: Potato, carrot, cucumber.

Good for: Cleansing.

Fig

Fresh figs make a very sweet, delicious juice that is a quick source of energy.

Pulp: Mix with carrot pulp for dessert topping.

Good source of: Potassium.

Combines well with: Apple, carrot.

Good for: Constipation.

Ginger Root

Here is another vegetable that can be kept relatively fresh for months and can be used as a minor ingredient in juices. Ginger root is often brewed as a tea to help soothe troubled stomachs.

Pulp: Use in salsas and pasta sauces.

Good source of: Vitamin B6, C; magnesium, and potassium.

Combines well with: Any other vegetable juice.

Good for: Relieving upset stomach.

Horseradish

If you like life on the hot side, you can warm up a juice drink (and open your sinuses) by adding a *small portion of horseradish* to your juice ingredients.

Pulp: Use in salsas and pasta sauces.

Good source of: Potassium and magnesium.

Combines well with: Any vegetable juice.

Good for: Treating stuffy heads, relieving water retention, and stimulating capillary function.

Caution: When juicing horseradish, wear some sort of protective eyewear, as the juice, if splashed in the eye, can be painful and may cause injury.

Jicama

Jicama is one of my favorite vegetables. It is a mild, tasty tuber that looks like a cross between a potato and a turnip. It can be cut into slices and eaten by itself or can be cut into strips and used in salads. For juicing, jicama makes a very good base to which you can add more strongly flavored vegetables. The juice from the jicama is mild, thick, and creamy, similar to potato juice. When you juice the jicama, wash it but do not peel it. Cut into slices that will fit into your juicer. The skin will be pulped away, but some of the vitamins and minerals that are present in or near the skin will be mixed into the juice to make it more nutritionally complete.

Pulp: Discard.

Good source of: Folate, vitamin C; potassium, and magnesium.

Combines well with: Carrot, cabbage, squash.

Good for: General cleansing.

Kiwi

The kiwi has become much easier to find and much less expensive over the past five years. It does not yield much juice, but what it does yield can be used to perk up other fruit juices. My writing partner, Richard, reports that he had fun mixing mango and kiwi fruit juice with carrot juice, which resulted in a very thick milkshake-like drink. (See recipe for Mango Joe.)

Pulp: Mix with other fruit pulp for dessert topping.

Good source of: Vitamin C; potassium and magnesium.

Combines well with: Apple, berry, mango, papaya.

Good for: General cleansing, colds and flu.

Leek

Leeks come from the same family as onions, but are much milder. When juiced, however, and used sparingly, they add a real zing to vegetable juices. From a nutritional standpoint, leeks are very powerful. Leek juice gives a nice lift to daikon radish juice or jicama juice. When juicing leeks, first remove the outer layer, as it is fibrous and can jam the juicer.

Pulp: Use in salsas and pasta sauces.

Good source of: Folate, C, and E; potassium, magnesium, iron.

Combines well with: Radish, jicama, carrot.

Good for: General cleansing.

Mango

This fruit is a bit difficult to work with because the pit in the middle clings tightly to the meat. Also, the mango meat does not juice very easily, and the juice that does come out is very thick. But the mango lends itself to enriching a thinner juice, such as apple. When you juice a mango, pick one that is still firm, on the early side of ripe, so that it is easier to work with. Cut the mango in half lengthwise, twist it apart, and then begin spooning the meat out into a bowl, discarding the skin. Trim as much of the meat as you can away from the pit, and discard the pit. Spoon the meat and the accumulated juice into the top of the juicer.

Pulp: Use as a topping for desserts, in muffins, cakes, and breads.

Good source of: Vitamin A, B6, C, E; potassium.

Combines well with: Apple, melon.

Good for: Colds and flu, digestion.

Papaya

Papaya meat is smooth and creamy and delicious. When juicing papayas, cut the fruit in half lengthwise and scoop out and discard the seeds; then scoop out the meat, discard the skin, and juice. Papaya is so thick and rich that you would do well to cut it with some lighter juice (such as apple) or with water.

Pulp: The bit of pulp you get from the meat can be used as a dessert topping or can be remixed with frozen papaya spears that you process through your juicer for a cool dessert.

Good source of: Vitamin A, C, folate; potassium. Contains beta-carotene, the cancer-fighter.

Combines well with: Cucumber, orange.

Good for: Cleansing various body systems, especially the kidneys and liver. Cut with apple juice or water, can help in weight loss. Has also been used to aid in curing ulcers. Very effective for easing constipation; papaya juice is my second favorite after fresh prune juice. Good weapon against cancer.

Rutabaga

Rutabagas are sometimes referred to as "Swedish turnips" and are essentially thick roots. Rutabagas produce a relatively mild juice.

Pulp: Discard.

Good source of: Folate and vitamin C, potassium, and magnesium.

Combines well with: Spinach, carrot, cabbage.

Good for: Cleansing liver, kidneys, bladder.

Tomatillo

The tomatillo looks like a dwarf green tomato. It has a very distinct, tart taste. I like to use it in salads. When you use the tomatillo for juicing (slice it first), mellow it with tomato juice or carrot juice. Tomatillos add a new dimension when you're experimenting with a half dozen or so vegetables.

Pulp: Use in pasta sauces.

Good source of: Vitamin A and C; calcium.

Combines well with: Spinach, cabbage.

Good for: Cleansing the bladder.

The Unjuiceables

When it comes to high-tech juicing, not all fruits and vegetables are created equal.

Most of the fruits and vegetables with which we are familiar lend themselves nicely to juicing. And many of the more exotic fruits and vegetables can also be juiced successfully.

There are, however, some fruits and vegetables that do not readily lend themselves to juicing, but can be incorporated in juices by using a simple household blender. There are also some fruits and vegetables that just plain don't work for juicing.

Avocado

The avocado is a favorite of mine. But like the banana, it has the wrong consistency to juice easily.

You can incorporate the avocado in your juicing by using the same method I describe below for the banana. Put a few strips of ripe avocado in your blender, pour in your fresh juice, and blend. The avocado will make the juice creamier and mellow some of the more powerful vegetables, such as cabbage. The avocado has a high fat content and should be used sparingly, but it is a store-house of eleven vitamins (especially A, D, and E) and seventeen minerals. And it is very high in beta-carotene, the cancer preventive.

Banana

The banana is another one of my favorite fruits. Bananas are a storehouse of potassium, and for anyone who leads an active life, potassium replacement is essential. This is why you see banana growers advertising so heavily in magazines aimed at long-distance runners and triath-letes. The problem with juicing bananas—or trying to—is that they gum up the juicer and produce almost no juice. But that doesn't mean you can't enjoy bananas as part of your juicing regimen—as long as you have a blender.

Pull out your blender and set it next to your juicer on the kitchen counter. Place a peeled, broken-up banana in the blender, and as soon as your favorite fruit juice comes out of the juicer, pour it into the blender with the banana, put on the top, and blend. The banana will make the juice creamier and thicker and will add that distinct banana flavor—as well as all those banana benefits: vitamin A, B-complex, C, and E.

The banana is perfect for mellowing some of the stronger fruits and for thickening your juices. (You'll find liberal use of bananas in the recipe section later in this book.)

The banana also makes a delightful dessert if you blend it with other fruit juices, pour the mixture into individual serving glasses or ice cream dishes, and par-tially freeze before serving.

Coconut

When it comes to juicing, coconut is better left alone. Besides producing little juice, coconut contains a lot of saturated fat. With the wide array of healthful fruits and vegetables you can juice easily, why fight with one that does not lend itself to juicing when it isn't very good for you anyway?

Eggplant

Although the eggplant can easily be juiced, it is very seldom used because its taste is bland and it contains few important nutrients relative to other vegetables.

Leek

Another vegetable favorite that is marginal for juicing is the leek. I love leeks and cook with them frequently. Their outer layers are difficult to juice, however, as they can often jam the juicing machine; before juicing, remove the outer layer. Also, leeks (like their relatives garlic and onions) are very potent, and should be used sparingly in juicing. They work wonderfully in adding a kick to a glass of mild vegetable juice.

Rhubarb

Rhubarb should be used sparingly, if at all, because of its high oxalic acid content. Oxalic acid combines with calcium in the body and forms crystals of calcium oxalate, which the body cannot use, thereby rendering the calcium useless.

Although you will hear from people that rhubarb is a good laxative, plenty of other fruits and vegetables can provide the same service without causing physical problems. On the rare occasions when I use rhubarb, I make it easier for the juicer to process by peeling off the outer skin and using only the softer central shaft. Never, ever use the green tops of rhubarb, as the oxalic acid is toxic in the leaves.

There are so many other good, safe fruits and vegetables available that it is easier just to skip rhubarb as a juice source.

Winter Squash

One of the best sources in the world of beta-carotene is the winter squash. Unfortunately, winter squash are generally very hard and are difficult enough to cut into pieces with a sharp knife, much less to juice. If you want to make a wonderful winter squash pulp that can be used in making squash bread (make it just as you'd make pumpkin or zucchini bread) while also extracting some squash juice you can use for your juicing, lightly steam precut chunks of winter squash that will fit into the port of your juicer, and then juice. The light steaming will soften up the squash. It will also make it necessary to use a spatula to collect the pulp from the top inside of the juicer, as it tends to stick to any surface it touches once it is softened. The summer squash lend themselves much better to juicing, and should be used frequently in your juicing regimen, even though their beta-carotene content is nowhere near that of the winter squash.

PART TWO

JUICING RECIPES

5

Recipes for Breakfast, Lunch, Dinner, and Parties

I can't even begin to tell you what a wonderful time I had putting together the recipes in this book. Don't think you *must* do your juicing recipes *exactly* as they are presented in this or any other juicing book. Experiment. Mix and match. Sometimes the result may not be the most delicious concoction in the world, but you can rest assured that since it's made from fresh fruits and vegetables, it's good for you. And you may surprise yourself by coming up with some delicious combinations that nobody's ever conceived before.

Remember that all you need to do to embark on your adventure is to raid the produce section of your supermarket, wash and trim and cut your fresh fruits and vegetables, set out some small glasses so that you can keep the juices separate until you have enough to mix and match, and keep a pad of paper handy so that you can record your inventions.

Eye-Openers

Most of us associate juices with breakfast. The most popular juice for celebrating the rising of the sun is orange juice. Tomato juice is also a standby at breakfast, and has long provided the basis for "eye-opener" drinks such as Bloody Marys. Also popular, especially with those who suffer from constipation, is prune juice, a natural laxative. Other "morning juices" include grapefruit and apple.

As I've discussed earlier, citrus juices, although crowd-pleasers, are not especially good for most people, since these juices are more difficult than others to metabolize.

All of the juices we associate with breakfast are fruit juices. My own favorite "eye-opener" is not a fruit juice, however, but carrot juice with celery. I've been using this simple, wonderful juice for decades to get my engine started in the morning.

A fresh glass of juice is a wonderful way to get any day off to a good start, but I'd like to suggest that you also eat a little something solid with your morning juice, even if it's a piece of dry whole-grain toast, to help absorb stomach acids that are produced when the stomach is activated.

Carrot Prime

. . . .

4 large carrots
1 large stalk celery, with top left on

1. Insert carrots into juicer; collect and set aside carrot pulp for later use in Simple Carrot Cake.
2. Insert celery.
3. Pour liquid into glass, stir, and drink.

YIELDS: 8 ounces.

GOOD SOURCE OF: Beta-carotene, vitamin A, B-complex, D, E, and K, iron, calcium, sodium, potassium, magnesium, and manganese.

GOOD FOR: Stomach ulcers, cancer prevention.

Morning Delight

· ·

1 large carrot
1 medium Red Delicious apple
1 pint fresh strawberries

1. Insert washed and unpeeled carrot; save pulp for later use.

2. Insert apple and save pulp for later use or enjoy as applesauce with breakfast.

3. Wash and hull strawberries and insert; save pulp for later use.

4. Stir juice and drink.

Hint: You can mix the pulp from all three ingredients and freeze to make sorbet.

YIELDS: 1¼ cups.

GOOD SOURCE OF: Beta-carotene; vitamin C, A, B-complex, D, E, and K; iron; calcium; sodium; potassium; phosphorus; and niacin.

GOOD FOR: Skin, cancer prevention.

Breakfast Treat

. . . .

4 pineapple slices
1 pink grapefruit, peeled but with white pith
   remaining

1. Juice pineapple, freezing pulp for later use.
2. Juice grapefruit.
3. Stir and drink.

YIELDS: 1½ cups.

GOOD SOURCE OF: Vitamin C, A, and B-complex; iodine; magnesium; manganese; potassium; and phosphorus.

GOOD FOR: Digestion, colds and flu.

Sunrise-Sunset

. . . .

3 slices pineapple
½ orange, peeled but with white pith remaining
4 fresh strawberries
1 bunch red grapes

1. Juice pineapple, freezing pulp for later use.
2. Juice other ingredients.
3. Stir and drink.

YIELDS: 1½ cups.

GOOD SOURCE OF: Vitamin C, A, and B-complex; iodine; magnesium; iron; sodium; phosphorus; and mucilage.

GOOD FOR: Colds and flu, general cleansing.

Pineapple-Orange Zing
. . . .

> *4 pineapple spears*
> *1 medium orange, peeled but with white pith*
> *remaining*

1. Juice pineapple spears, freezing pulp for later use.
2. Juice orange.
3. Stir and drink.

YIELDS: 1 cup.

GOOD SOURCE OF: Vitamin C, A, and B-complex; iodine; magnesium; manganese; and calcium.

GOOD FOR: Digestion, colds and flu.

Pineapple-Pear Zing
. . . .

> *4 pineapple spears*
> *1 medium pear*

1. Juice pineapple, freeezing pulp for later use.
2. Juice pear, freezing pulp for later use.
3. Stir and drink.

YIELDS: 1 cup.

GOOD SOURCE OF: Vitamin C, A, B1, and B2; phosphorus; sodium; calcium; magnesium; sulfur; and potassium.

GOOD FOR: Constipation, general cleansing.

Broccoli Blast

. . . .

½ pineapple, skin removed, cut into spears
1 large head broccoli, stalks removed, flowerets
separated

Juice both ingredients, saving pulp for later use. Stir thoroughly.

YIELDS: 1½ cups.

GOOD SOURCE OF: Vitamin A, B-complex, and C; riboflavin; iron; calcium; iodine; magnesium; manganese; potassium; phosphorus; and sulfur.

GOOD FOR: Colds and flu, cancer prevention.

Vitamin C Punch

. . . .

1 pink grapefruit, peeled but with white pith
remaining
½ pineapple, skin removed, cut into spears
1 lemon, peeled but with white pith remaining

1. Juice all ingredients, saving pulp for later use.
2. Pour juice into pitcher filled with ice, stir, and
serve.

YIELDS: 3 cups.

GOOD SOURCE OF: Vitamin A, B-complex, C, and P; calcium;
phosphorus; iodine; magnesium; manganese; potassium;
iron; and sulfur.

GOOD FOR: Weight loss, colds and flu.

Berry Blizzard

. . . .

1 pound cranberries, thoroughly washed, stems
*   removed*
2 pounds raspberries, rinsed
2 medium oranges, peeled but with white pith
*   remaining*

1. Juice cranberries and raspberries, saving combined pulp for Berry Blizzard Topping.
2. Juice oranges.
3. Serve over crushed or shaved ice.

YIELDS: 4 cups.

GOOD SOURCE OF: Vitamin A, C, and P; calcium; and phosphorus.

GOOD FOR: Digestion, general cleansing.

Blackberry-Apple Delight

. . . .

2 large sweet apples
½ pint blackberries, rinsed

1. Juice apples, then blackberries, saving pulp mixture for Blackberry Applesauce.
2. Serve juice over ice.

YIELDS: 1½ cups.

GOOD SOURCE OF: Vitamin B1, B2, B6, and C; and niacin.

GOOD FOR: Skin and hair, general cleansing.

Breakfast Punch

....

*1 2-inch-thick slice of watermelon cut from half
melon*
¼ pineapple, skin removed, cut into spears
*1 medium orange, peeled but with white pith
remaining*
2 heaping tablespoons protein powder

1. Juice watermelon, pineapple, and orange.
2. Add protein powder.
3. Stir well or mix in blender and serve.

YIELDS: 2 cups.

GOOD SOURCE OF: Protein; vitamin A, B-complex, C, and P;
iodine; magnesium; manganese; potassium; calcium;
phosphorus; iron; sulfur; and cellulose.

GOOD FOR: Digestion, general cleansing.

Up and At 'Em

. . . .

6 large carrots
1 medium beet

1. Juice carrots, saving pulp for later use.
2. Juice beets.
3. Stir and drink.

YIELDS: 1½ cups.

GOOD SOURCE OF: Beta-carotene; vitamin A, B-complex, C, D, E, and K; iron; calcium; sodium; potassium; magnesium; manganese; sulfur; copper; and phosphorus.

GOOD FOR: Urinary tract, cancer prevention.

Carrot-Fruit Juice

. . . .

4 large carrots
2 sweet apples, such as Red or Golden
    Delicious

Juice both ingredients, saving mixed pulp for later use as fruit topping or Apple-Carrot Sauce.

YIELDS: 1¼ cups.

GOOD SOURCE OF: Beta-carotene; vitamin A, B-complex, C, D, E, and K; iron; calcium; sodium; potassium; magnesium; manganese; sulfur; copper; phosphorus; and niacin.

GOOD FOR: Skin and hair, cancer prevention.

Apri-Cran Juice
. . . .

2 pounds cranberries
1½ pounds apricots (remove skin if your
machine has difficulty handling apricot or
peach skins)
¼ lemon, peeled but with white pith remaining
2 cups crushed ice

1. Juice all fruit ingredients, saving pulp for Apri-Cran Topping.
2. Stir juice and pour over ice.

YIELDS: 2½ cups.

GOOD SOURCE OF: Beta-carotene; vitamin A, B, C, and P; protein; calcium; and phosphorus.

GOOD FOR: General cleansing, cancer prevention.

Sunrise

....

2 sweet apples
4 large carrots
1 red bell pepper
4 jicama spears

1. Juice apples and carrots, saving pulp for Apple-Carrot Sauce.
2. Juice remaining ingredients. Stir and drink.

YIELDS: 2 cups.

GOOD SOURCE OF: Vitamin A, B-complex, C, D, E, and K; iron; calcium; sodium; potassium; magnesium; manganese; sulfur; copper; phosphorus; and niacin.

GOOD FOR: Eyes, skin, hair, digestion, stomach ulcers, colds, and flu, general cleansing/detoxifying; cancer prevention.

A.M. Blend

· ·

1 cup strawberries
½ pineapple, cut into spears
1 cup orange juice

1. Juice strawberries and save pulp for breakfast or frozen yogurt topping.
2. Juice pineapple and save pulp for breakfast or dessert topping.
3. Mix ingredients together and drink.

YIELDS: 2½ cups.

GOOD SOURCE OF: Vitamin A, B-complex, C, E, and K; iron; sodium; phosphorus; magnesium; potassium; sulfur; manganese; calcium; silicon; iodine; and bromine.

GOOD FOR: Skin, muscle fatigue, rheumatism, and gout, constipation, colds and flu.

Chuck's Wake-Up

. . . .

½ cucumber
½ bell pepper
1 large carrot
1 stalk celery
1 sweet apple
1 zucchini
1 tomato
2 or 3 yellow pepperoncinis

Juice all ingredients, stir thoroughly, and drink immediately.

YIELDS: 2 cups.

GOOD SOURCE OF: Vitamin A, B-complex, C, D, E, and K; iron; calcium; sodium; potassium; magnesium; manganese; sulfur; copper; silicon; iodine; and phosphorus.

GOOD FOR: Eyes, skin, "bad breath," and digestion, general cleansing, ulcers, arthritis, cancer prevention.

Liquid Lunches

If you've had an adequate breakfast (a glass of juice and a piece of toast, for example, or whole-grain pancakes and some juice), you probably can afford to have a liquid lunch. By having a nutritious glass of juice for lunch, you'll give your body a good shot of fresh vitamins and minerals, and your stomach won't have to work so hard to process lunch.

This liquid lunch will have two positive effects: It will cut down on your calorie intake, and it will help keep the blood flowing to your brain for the rest of the day so that you won't suffer that energy lapse in the middle of the afternoon when all you can think about is lying down to take a nap.

Try some of these delicious liquid lunches as a pleasant change of pace.

V-6 Power Lunch
. . . .

4 *medium tomatoes, washed and quartered*
  lengthwise
2 *large carrots, washed and unpeeled, halved*
  lengthwise
½ *head cabbage, wedged for each easy*
  insertion into machine
2 *large stalks celery, with tops, halved*
  lengthwise
1 *medium turnip, with skin, quartered*
1 *head broccoli, stalk removed, flowerets*
  separated
½ *lemon without skin, sliced lengthwise in a*
  wedge

1. Process tomatoes first; collect pulp and set aside for later use in pasta sauce or salsa.
2. Add other ingredients.
3. Pour 16 ounces into glass and drink.
4. Share other half of recipe with a friend. If you are making the recipe for yourself alone, cut ingredients in half.

Suggestion: Serve over ice, with upper half of celery stalk riding in glass.

YIELDS: 32 ounces (2 generous servings).

GOOD SOURCE OF: Beta-carotene; vitamin A, B1, B2, B6, C, and K; phosphorus; potassium; iron; bromine; calcium; sodium; magnesium; iodine; and copper.

GOOD FOR: Ulcers, general cleansing.

Note: The wedge of lemon is added to provide a natural preservative in case you wish to refrigerate some of this juice for use a few hours later. Remember, however, that the longer you store juices, the more nutrients they lose; and the cabbage in this juice gives it limited refrigerator life.

Broccoli Bush

. . . .

4 medium carrots
½ medium green bell pepper
2 stalks broccoli

1. Juice carrots, saving pulp for later use.
2. Juice pepper, saving pulp for salsa.
3. Juice heads of broccoli, discarding stalk.
4. Stir juice and drink.

YIELDS: 1 cup

GOOD SOURCE OF: Beta-carotene; vitamin A and C; riboflavin; iron; calcium; sodium; potassium; magnesium; manganese; and copper.

GOOD FOR: General cleansing, cancer prevention.

Cool Head Luke

•••

1 large Red Delicious apple
3 medium carrots
¼ medium cucumber, peeled
½ large head broccoli

1. Juice apple and carrots, saving pulp for Apple-Carrot Sauce.
2. Juice cucumber and broccoli.
3. Mix all juices and drink.

YIELDS: 1 cup.

GOOD SOURCE OF: Vitamin A, B-complex, C, D, E, and K; iron; calcium; sodium; potassium; magnesium; manganese; sulfur; copper; and phosphorus.

GOOD FOR: Weight loss, general cleansing.

Vital C Punch

· ·

3 large tomatoes
2 medium oranges, peeled but with white pith
    remaining
½ pineapple, skin removed, cut into spears

1. Juice tomatoes, saving pulp for salsa or pasta sauce.
2. Juice pineapple, saving pulp for later use.
3. Juice oranges.
4. Stir all juices together and serve with or without ice.

YIELDS: 3½ cups.

GOOD SOURCE OF: Vitamin A, B1, B2, B6, C, and K; phosphorus; potassium; iron; bromine; iodine; magnesium; manganese; calcium; and sulfur.

GOOD FOR: Digestion, general cleansing.

Tummy Salad

. . . .

3 medium carrots
¼ head cabbage, sliced to fit into juicer
1 stalk celery
5 sweet cherries, pitted

1. Juice carrots, celery, and cabbage, saving pulp for Cole Slaw.
2. Juice cherries.
3. Stir juices together and drink.

YIELDS: 1¼ cups.

GOOD SOURCE OF: Beta-carotene; vitamin A, B-complex, C, D, E, and K; iron; calcium; sodium; potassium; magnesium; sulfur; copper; phosphorus; and iodine.

GOOD FOR: Ulcers, cancer prevention.

Top 10 Juice

. . . .

1 large tomato
3 large carrots
½ red bell pepper
½ green bell pepper
½ yellow bell pepper
1 small onion
2 stalks celery, including tops
¼ head iceberg lettuce
1 small cucumber, skinned
2 ounces fennel juices (ready-made or made
      with a wheatgrass juicer)

1. Juice tomato, carrots, bell peppers, onion, and celery, saving pulp for salsa.

2. Juice lettuce and cucumber.

3. Stir together with fennel juice and drink immediately.

YIELDS: 2½ to 3 cups.

GOOD SOURCE OF: Beta-carotene; vitamin A, B-complex, C, D, E, and K; phosphorus; potassium; iron; bromine; calcium; sodium; magnesium; manganese; sulfur; copper; iodine; cobalt; and zinc.

GOOD FOR: Ulcers, lowering blood pressure.

Tomato Salsa Drink

. . . .

1 tablespoon fresh crumbled cilantro
2 large tomatoes
1 small onion
2 jalapeño peppers
½ lime, peeled but with white pith remaining

1. Run cilantro through juicer first so that additional ingredients pick up cilantro flavor as they are processed.
2. Juice tomatoes, onion, and peppers.
3. Juice lime.
4. Save pulp of all ingredients combined for Salsa Salsa.
5. Stir juices together and drink.

YIELDS: 2 cups.

GOOD SOURCE OF: Vitamin A, B1, B2, B6, C, and K; phosphorus; potassium; iron; and bromine.

GOOD FOR: Weight loss, general cleansing.

The Lunch Bucket

· ·

2 medium sweet apples
1 cucumber, peeled
1 yellow summer squash
1 zucchini
1 stalk celery

1. Juice apples, saving pulp for later use.
2. Juice vegetables.
3. Stir and serve over ice.

YIELDS: 2 cups.

GOOD SOURCE OF: Vitamin A, B-complex, and C; iron; silicon; sulfur; manganese; potassium; sodium; calcium; phosphorus; magnesium; niacin; iodine; and copper.

GOOD FOR: General cleansing, cancer prevention.

The Green Drink

. . . .

2 green apples
4 stalks celery
8 stalks bok choy (Chinese cabbage)
¼ pound spinach
1 bunch parsley

Juice all ingredients and stir thoroughly.

YIELDS: 2 cups.

GOOD SOURCE OF: Vitamin A, B-complex, and C; sodium; magnesium; manganese; iron; iodine; copper; potassium; calcium; phosphorus; niacin; and chlorine.

GOOD FOR: Hair and skin, bad breath, colds and flu, digestion and weight loss, gout, cancer prevention; general cleansing.

Johann S. Bok

. . . .

¼ pound bok choy
2 sweet apples
3 large carrots
1 red bell pepper

1. Juice the apples and carrots together, saving pulp for Apple-Carrot Sauce.
2. Juice remaining ingredients and stir thoroughly.

YIELDS: 2 cups.

GOOD SOURCE OF: Vitamin A, B-complex, C, D, E, K; iron; calcium; sodium; potassium; magnesium; manganese; sulfur; copper; phosphorus; and niacin.

GOOD FOR: Eyes, skin, hair; appetite, digestion, general cleansing/detoxifying, colds and flu; cancer prevention.

The Color Orange

. . . .

1 cantaloupe, skinned
2 large carrots
½ lime, peeled but with white pith remaining

Juice all ingredients, stir, and drink.

YIELDS: 3 cups.

GOOD SOURCE OF: Vitamin A, B-complex, C, D, E, and K; iron; calcium; sodium; potassium; magnesium; manganese; sulfur; copper; phosphorus; and cellulose.

GOOD FOR: Eyes and skin, stomach ulcers; general cleansing, digestion, cancer prevention.

The Stomach Soother

. . . .

½ head cabbage
1 beet with greens
2 large kiwis

1. Juice cabbage first, saving pulp for Cole Slaw.
2. Juice beet and save pulp for later use.
3. Juice kiwis and mix all juices together.

YIELDS: 2⅓ cups.

GOOD SOURCE OF: Vitamins A, B-complex, and C; potassium; sulfur; calcium; phosphorus; and iodine.

GOOD FOR: Skin, hair, heart, blood pressure, and circulation, digestion and ulcers, general cleansing.

Energy, Please!

As I mentioned earlier, people often find that they have an energy lapse midway through the afternoon. If your diet is good and you had a light lunch, this dip in energy means that you've burned up some of your energy reserves. It is a natural phenomenon. The lapse may be more acute if you ate a large lunch, since the stomach must spend a terrific amount of energy processing the food, thereby diverting blood and oxygen from the brain.

Television commercials would have us believe that what we need to give us a midafternoon lift is a candy bar. Nothing could be further from the truth! A candy bar will provide a temporary lift—and a very predictable drop in energy soon thereafter that will leave you more tired than you were before you ate the candy.

Instead of wasting your time on such temporary solutions, try one of these drinks for quick—and sustained—energy.

Energybomb

· ·

5 large carrots
3 medium Red Delicious apples
1 tablespoon citrus-flavored powdered athletic
   fluid replacement drink mix

1. Feed carrots into juicer and save pulp for later use.
2. Feed apples into juicer and save pulp for later use.
3. Stir juice while mixing in drink mix.

YIELDS: 1½ cups.

GOOD SOURCE OF: Beta-carotene; vitamin A, B-complex, C, D, E, and K; iron; calcium; sodium; potassium; and electrolytes.

GOOD FOR: Skin and hair, cancer prevention.

The Vitamin Whiz

. . . .

3 medium carrots
30 pitted Bing cherries
1 large orange, peeled but white pith remaining
10 ounces bottled mineral water

1. Juice carrots, saving pulp for later use.
2. Juice cherries, freezing pulp for dessert topping.
3. Juice orange.
4. Stir juices together, then pour in mineral water.

YIELDS: 2 cups.

GOOD SOURCE OF: Beta-carotene; vitamin C, B-complex, D, E, and K; iron; calcium; sodium; potassium; magnesium; and trace minerals.

GOOD FOR: Skin and hair, cancer prevention.

Big Red

· ·

2 medium carrots
1 large red bell pepper
2 small Red Delicious apples

1. Juice carrots, saving pulp for later use.
2. Juice pepper, saving pulp for salsa or pasta sauce.
3. Juice apples, saving pulp for later use.
4. Stir and drink.

YIELDS: 1 cup.

GOOD SOURCE OF: Beta-carotene; vitamin A, B-complex, C, E, and K; iron; calcium; sodium; potassium; and magnesium.

GOOD FOR: Regularity, cancer prevention.

Melon Mania

. . . .

¼ *honeydew, skinned and cut into spears*
¼ *orange-fleshed honeydew, skinned and cut*
    into spears
¼ *Crenshaw melon, skinned and cut into*
    spears
¼ *cantaloupe, skinned and cut into spears*
¼ *pineapple, skin removed, cut into spears*
⅛ *medium watermelon, skinned and cut into*
    spears
10 *strawberries, minus stems*

1. Juice all ingredients, pouring juice into pitcher as needed to keep machine's juice container from overflowing.
2. Stir and serve.

YIELDS: 6 cups.

GOOD SOURCE OF: Vitamin A, B-complex, C, E, and K; iron; sodium; phosphorus; magnesium; potassium; sulfur; calcium; silicon; iodine; and bromine.

GOOD FOR: Skin, general cleansing.

Melontasia

. . . .

*1 medium orange, peeled but with white pith
    remaining
¼ honeydew, skinned and cut into spears
¼ cantaloupe, skinned and cut into spears*

Juice all ingredients, stir, and drink.

YIELDS: 1¼ cups.

GOOD SOURCE OF: Vitamin A, B1, C, and P; cellulose; calcium; and phosphorus.

GOOD FOR: Colds and flu, general cleansing.

Strawberry Surprise

. . . .

*¼ pineapple, skin removed, cut into spears
10 strawberries
1 head broccoli*

1. Juice pineapple and strawberries and save pulp for use as fruit topping.
2. Juice broccoli flowerets; peel stalk and juice.
3. Stir all ingredients and drink.

YIELDS: 1 cup.

GOOD SOURCE OF: Vitamin A, B-complex, C, E, and K; iron; sodium; phosphorus; magnesium; potassium; sulfur; calcium; silicon; iodine; and bromine.

GOOD FOR: Digestion, sore muscles.

Apple Pucker

. . . .

1 large green Granny Smith apple
3 stalks celery

Juice ingredients and serve over ice.

YIELDS: 1 cup.

GOOD SOURCE OF: Vitamin A, B-complex, and C; sodium; magnesium; manganese; iron; iodine; copper, potassium; calcium; and phosphorus.

GOOD FOR: Hair and skin, general cleansing.

Pineapple Zip

. . . .

½ pineapple, skin removed, cut into spears
½ pound sweet grapes
½ cantaloupe, skinned and cut into spears

1. Juice pineapple, saving pulp for later use.
2. Juice grapes and cantaloupe.
3. Stir juices and drink.

YIELDS: 3 cups.

GOOD SOURCE OF: Vitamin A, B-complex, and C; iodine; magnesium; manganese; potassium; calcium; phosphorus; iron; and sulfur.

GOOD FOR: Colds and flu, general cleansing.

Cilantro Squirt

. . . .

1 tablespoon fresh cilantro leaves
2 medium tomatoes
1 small onion

1. Run cilantro leaves through juicer.
2. Juice tomatoes and onion, saving pulp for salsa.

YIELDS: 1 cup.

GOOD SOURCE OF: Vitamin A, B1, B2, B6, C, and K; phosphorus; potassium; iron; and bromine.

GOOD FOR: Skin, general cleansing.

Pine-Straw Juice

. . . .

¼ pineapple, skin removed, cut into spears
½ pint strawberries, stems removed

1. Juice ingredients, saving pulp for Pine-Straw Topping.
2. Pour into closed container, shake, and serve over ice.

YIELDS: 1½ cups.

GOOD SOURCE OF: Vitamin A, B-complex, C, E, and K; iron; sodium; phosphorus; magnesium; potassium; calcium; silicon; iodine; bromine; manganese; and sulfur.

GOOD FOR: Regularity, colds and flu.

Triple Grape Juice

. . . .

½ pound red seedless grapes
½ pound green seedless grapes
½ pound purple grapes

Juice all ingredients, stir, and serve over ice.

YIELDS: 1½ cups.

GOOD SOURCE OF: Mucilage; malic acid; tannin; and volatile acid.

GOOD FOR: Digestion, general cleansing.

Carrot-Cake Juice

. . . .

4 large carrots
¼ pineapple, skin removed, cut into spears
1 Golden Delicious apple
Ground cinnamon
Ground cardamom

1. Juice all three fruits, saving pulp for Carrot-Pineapple Sauce.
2. Stir juice and sprinkle cinnamon and cardamom on top to taste.

YIELDS: 2 cups.

GOOD SOURCE OF: Beta-carotene; vitamin A, B-complex, C, D, E, and K; iron; calcium; sodium; potassium; magnesium; manganese; sulfur; copper; phosphorus; niacin; and iodine.

GOOD FOR: Ulcers, cancer prevention.

The Beet Goes On

. . . .

4 medium carrots
2 stalks celery
1 beet, with hard segment where greens are
    attached removed

1. Juice carrots and celery first, saving pulp for later use.
2. Juice beet.
3. Stir and drink.

YIELDS: 1 cup.

GOOD SOURCE OF: Beta-carotene; vitamin A, B-complex, C, D, E, and K; iron; calcium; sodium; potassium; magnesium; manganese; sulfur; copper; and iodine.

GOOD FOR: Urinary tract, ulcers.

Potato Power

. . . .

4 medium potatoes, with skins
4 medium carrots
1 stalk broccoli
6 brussels sprouts
1 cucumber, peeled

1. Juice potatoes, saving pulp for Potato-Apple Pancakes.
2. Juice carrots, saving pulp for later use.
3. Juice remaining vegetables, stir, and drink.

YIELDS: 4 cups.

GOOD SOURCE OF: Beta-carotene; vitamin A, B-complex, C, D, E, and K; iron; calcium; sodium; potassium; magnesium; manganese; sulfur; copper; phosphorus; iodine; protein; carbohydrates; ribloflavin; and silicon.

GOOD FOR Ulcers, general cleansing.

The Pepper-Upper

. . . .

1 green bell pepper
1 red bell pepper
1 sweet apple
2 large carrots

1. Juice bell peppers together and save for pulp recipes.

2. Juice apple and carrots together, saving pulp for Apple-Carrot Sauce.

3. Thoroughly stir all juices and drink.

YIELDS: 2 cups.

GOOD SOURCE OF: Vitamin A, B-complex, C, D, E, and K; iron; calcium; sodium; potassium; magnesium; manganese; sulfur; copper; phosphorus; and niacin.

GOOD FOR: Eyes, skin, hair, and heart, ulcers and digestion, colds and flu, helps colitis, detoxifying, cancer prevention.

Beta Belt

. . . .

2 medium carrots
1 medium yellow summer squash
2 large plums

1. Juice carrots and save pulp for variety of uses.
2. Juice squash and save for pulp recipes.
3. Juice plums and mix all juices together thoroughly.

YIELDS: 1½ cups.

GOOD SOURCE OF: Vitamin A, B-complex, C, D, E, and K; iron; calcium; sodium; potassium; magnesium; manganese; sulfur; copper; and phosphorus.

GOOD FOR: Eyes and skin, ulcers and digestion, appetite stimulant, general cleansing, cancer prevention.

Pineapple Power

· ·

1 pineapple, skin removed, cut into spears
4 large carrots
½ lemon, peeled but with white pith remaining
½ lime, peeled but with white pith remaining

1. Juice pineapple first and save pulp for breakfast or dessert topping.
2. Juice carrots and save pulp for a variety of uses.
3. Juice citrus and mix all juices together.

YIELDS: 3 cups.

GOOD SOURCE OF: Vitamin A, B-complex, C, D, E, and K; sodium; copper; iodine; magnesium; manganese; potassium; calcium; phosphorus; iron; and sulfur.

GOOD FOR: Eyes and skin, ulcers and digestion, colds and flu, cancer prevention.

Apple Pie Drink

. . . .

½ teaspoon nutmeg
½ teaspoon cinnamon
4 large sweet apples
1 large carrot

1. Before beginning to juice, sprinkle nutmeg and cinnamon into juicer.
2. Juice apples and carrot, saving pulp for another recipe.
3. Drink juice immediately. Can be served over ice.

YIELDS: 2 cups.

GOOD SOURCE OF: Beta-carotene; vitamin A, B-complex, C, D, E, and K; iron; calcium; sodium; potassium; magnesium; manganese; sulfur; copper; phosphorus; and niacin.

GOOD FOR: Eyes, skin and hair, ulcers, regularity, detoxifying, colds and flu.

Evening Enliveners

After breakfast, the evening meal is usually the most important of the day—and the one during which the average person takes in more calories than at any other meal.

The fruit or vegetable drink you have with your evening meal can be diluted with water to make it go farther, help you get your daily requirement of fluids, and cut calories.

The Kitchen Sink

. . . .

> *2 large carrots*
> *2 small Red Delicious apples*
> *2 stalks celery*
> *2 broccoli flowerets*
> *⅓ medium cucumber, peeled*

1. Juice carrots, saving pulp for later use.
2. Juice apples, saving pulp for later use.
3. Juice celery, broccoli, and cucumber.
4. Stir and drink.

   YIELDS: 1¼ cups.

   GOOD SOURCE OF: Beta-carotene; vitamin A, B-complex, C, D, E; iron; riboflavin; calcium; and sulfur.

   GOOD FOR: Ulcers, general cleansing, cancer prevention.

Sweet Deluxe

. . . .

2 stalks celery
1 large tomato
1 red bell pepper
1 large carrot
1 small Red Delicious apple
½ medium cucumber

1. Juice celery, tomato, and pepper and save pulp for salsa.

2. Juice carrot and apple and mix pulp for Apple-Carrot Sauce.

3. Juice cucumber.

4. Stir together and drink.

YIELDS: 1 cup.

GOOD SOURCE OF: Beta-carotene; vitamin A, B-complex, C, D, E, and K; iron; calcium; sodium; potassium; magnesium, manganese, phosphorus, and bromine.

GOOD FOR: Lowering blood pressure, general cleansing.

Beet Treat

. . . .

4 medium carrots
1 beet, with hard section where greens are
*   attached removed*
½ medium cucumber
1 stalk celery

1. Juice carrots and save pulp for later use.
2. Juice beet, cucumber, and celery.
3. Stir and drink.

YIELDS: 1½ cups.

GOOD SOURCE OF: Beta-carotene; vitamin A, B-complex, C, D, E, and K; iron, phosphorus; sulfur; potassium; sodium; magnesium; and manganese.

GOOD FOR: Urinary tract, ulcers.

Beta-Apple Lite
· ·

3 medium Red or Golden Delicious apples
3 medium carrots
¼ lemon, peeled but with white pith remaining

1. Juice all ingredients, saving pulp for Apple-Carrot Sauce.
2. Stir juices and drink.

YIELDS: 1½ cups.

GOOD SOURCE OF: Beta-carotene; vitamin A, B-complex, C, D, E, and K; iron; calcium; sodium; potassium; magnesium; manganese; sulfur; copper; and phosphorus.

GOOD FOR: Hair and skin, cancer prevention.

Orangeade
· ·

4 medium oranges, peeled but with white pith
remaining
¼ lime, peeled but with white pith remaining
½ lemon, peeled but with white pith remaining
1 cup water

Feed fruits through juicer, stir into water, and pour over ice.

GOOD SOURCE OF: Vitamin A, C, and P; calcium; and phosphorus.

GOOD FOR: Digestion, colds and flu.

Hot Cooler
· ·

1 large cucumber, peeled
1 small onion

Juice ingredients, stir, and drink.

YIELDS: 1 cup.

GOOD SOURCE OF: Vitamin A, B-complex, and C; iron; silicon; sulfur; manganese; potassium; sodium; calcium; and phosphorus.

GOOD FOR: Skin, general cleansing.

Potato Milk
· ·

3 medium potatoes, with skins
4 medium carrots
1 medium white radish

1. Juice potatoes, saving pulp for Potato-Apple Pancakes.
2. Juice carrots, saving pulp for later use.
3. Juice radish.
4. Mix all juices and drink.

YIELDS: 2 cups.

GOOD SOURCE OF: Beta-carotene; vitamin A, B-complex, C, D, E, K, and P; iron; calcium; sodium; potassium, magnesium; manganese; sulfur; copper; phosphorus; iodine; protein; and carbohydrates.

GOOD FOR: Skin, general cleansing.

Rainbow Juice

• •

> 1 stalk celery
> 4 medium carrots
> 1 cucumber, peeled
> 1 yellow summer squash
> 1 medium zucchini
> 4 medium carrots
> 1 sweet apple

1. Juice carrots and celery and save pulp for later use.

2. Juice remaining vegetables, stir, and serve over ice.

YIELDS: 2 cups.

GOOD SOURCE OF: Vitamin A, B-complex, and C; iron; silicon; sulfur; manganese; potassium; sodium; calcium; phosphorus; magnesium; niacin; iodine, and copper.

GOOD FOR: General cleansing, cancer prevention.

Up Juice

. . . .

4 medium carrots
2 stalks celery
1 beet, with hard segment where greens are
     attached removed
1 sweet apple
1 stalk asparagus

1. Juice carrots and celery and save pulp for later use.
2. Juice beet, apple, and asparagus.
3. Stir and drink.

YIELDS: 1½ cups.

GOOD SOURCE OF: Beta-carotene; vitamin A, B-complex, C, D, E, and K; iron; calcium; sodium; potassium; magnesium; manganese; sulfur; copper; phosphorus; iodine; and niacin.

GOOD FOR: Urinary tract, weight loss.

Chuck's Mix

. . . .

1 orange, peeled but with white pith remaining
1 sweet apple
1 large carrot
1 grapefruit, peeled but with white pith
    remaining
1 pear or ½ cantaloupe

1. Juice apple and carrot and save pulp for Apple-Carrot Sauce.

2. Juice remaining ingredients and mix.

YIELDS: 3 cups.

GOOD SOURCE OF: Vitamin A, B-complex, C, D, E, and K; iron; calcium; sodium; potassium; magnesium; manganese; sulfur; copper; phosphorus; and cellulose.

GOOD FOR: Eyes, skin, and hair, colds and flu, regularity; general cleansing, cancer prevention.

Summertime

. . . .

2 large cucumbers, peeled
2 large carrots
1 sweet apple
½ lemon, peeled but with white pith remaining

1. Juice carrots, then juice apple; saving pulp for Apple-Carrot Sauce.
2. Juice cucumbers and lemon.
3. Mix all juices together and drink.

YIELDS: 3 cups.

GOOD SOURCE OF: Vitamin A, B-complex, C, D, E, and K; iron; silicon; sulfur; manganese; potassium; sodium; calcium; phosphorus; magnesium; and copper.

GOOD FOR: Eyes and skin, ulcers and blood pressure, regularity, general cleansing, cancer prevention.

Delicious Desserts

One of the wonderful benefits of the modern high-speed centrifugal juicers is that the same fruits and vegetables you use to make delicious, nutritious juices can also make wonderful desserts that you can enjoy without the slightest guilt.

Bob's Delight

. . . .

> *1 scoop frozen vanilla yogurt*
> *1 ounce watermelon juice*
> *1 ounce pineapple juice*
> *1 ounce cantaloupe juice*
> *2 to 3 sliced strawberries*

1. Scoop frozen vanilla yogurt into sundae dish.
2. Pour three juices over yogurt.
3. Top with sliced strawberries.

YIELDS: 1 sundae.

GOOD SOURCE OF: Vitamin A, B-complex, and C; iodine; magnesium; manganese; potassium; calcium; phosphorus; iron; sulfur; and cellulose.

GOOD FOR: Colds and flu, general cleansing.

Summer Melon Medley

⅛ medium watermelon, skinned, cut into
    spears
¼ Crenshaw melon, skinned, cut into spears
¼ cantaloupe, skinned, cut into spears
12 strawberries, stems removed
2 pitted apricots (with skins removed if your
    juicer has trouble handling apricot or peach
    skins)

1. Juice strawberries and apricots, saving pulp for
later use.
2. Juice all melons.
3. Stir juices together and serve over ice.

YIELDS: 2½ cups.

GOOD SOURCE OF: Beta-carotene; vitamin A, B-complex, C,
E, and K; iron; sodium; phosphorus; magnesium; potassium; calcium; silicon; iodine; bromine; cellulose; and
protein.

GOOD FOR: Skin, detoxifying.

Pineapple Turbo

• •

1 pineapple, skin removed, cut into spears

1. Juice pineapple, saving pulp for Pineapple Sauce.
2. Serve over ice in tall glass that has been frozen in freezer.

YIELDS: 3 cups.

GOOD SOURCE OF: Vitamin A, B-complex, and C; iodine; magnesium; manganese; potassium; calcium; phosphorus; iron; and sulfur.

GOOD FOR: Digestion, colds and flu.

Apple Turbo

• •

5 large sweet apples

1. Juice apples, saving pulp for later use.
2. Serve over ice in tall glass that has been frozen in freezer.

YIELDS: 3 cups.

GOOD SOURCE OF: Vitamin B1, B2, and B6; and niacin.

GOOD FOR: Hair and skin, detoxifying.

Raspberry Rush
. . . .

½ pound raspberries
1 large orange, peeled but with white pith
     remaining
1 medium lime, peeled but with white pith
     remaining

1. Juice raspberries, saving pulp to mix with apple pulp to make Rasplesauce.
2. Juice orange and lime and mix with raspberry juice. Serve over crushed ice.

YIELDS: 1¼ cups.

GOOD SOURCE OF: Vitamin A, C, and P; calcium; and phosphorus.

GOOD FOR: Appetite, regularity.

Party Perfect

Freshly juiced fruit lends itself to a variety of refreshing and exciting drinks of the type you might be served on a vacation in the tropics.

Over the past few years, I've enjoyed putting together freshly juiced fancy drinks, with and without alcohol, for dinner guests. They can't get over the lively taste. I often add some of my favorite ingredient, carrot juice, to drinks that most people would not expect to find carrots in. Friends can't believe that the "magic" ingredient they can't quite place is carrot.

What follows is a set of recipes for everything from margaritas to piña coladas, including some you won't find in any bartender's guide. But remember, you don't need to stick to my recipes. Try different formulas, and have fun thinking up names for the drinks you concoct.

Strawberry Margarita
. . . .

6 large frozen fresh strawberries, or 10 medium frozen fresh strawberries, or a like amount of unsweetened *packaged frozen strawberries*
½ lime, cut lengthwise in wedges, skin removed
¼ orange, cut lengthwise in wedges, skin removed
1 ice cube, crushed or split to fit into machine
1 ounce tequila, optional

1. Freeze fresh strawberries a day in advance.
2. Juice remaining ingredients.
3. Combine juice and pulp, along with tequila, if desired.
4. Pour into frosted glass. (Salt the rims, if desired, before pouring into glass.)

YIELDS: 1 cup.

GOOD SOURCE OF: Vitamin A, B-complex, C, E, K, and P; calcium; phosphorus; iron; sodium; magnesium; potassium; sulfur; silicon; iodine; and bromine.

GOOD FOR: Skin, regularity.

Mango Joe

. . . .

> *1 firm, ripe mango*
> *2 kiwi fruits, unpeeled*
> *1 large carrot*
> *5 ounces sparkling mineral water or*
> *champagne*

1. Slice mango in half lengthwise over bowl (to catch juice). Twist to separate from pit. Use knife to cut off meat that sticks to pit. Use spoon to scoop out mango meat. Cut into slices and feed into juicer.

2. Add washed unpeeled kiwi fruits and carrot.

3. Stir to blend into creamy milkshake consistency.

4. Stir pulp and freeze for later use.

5. Pour drink into large glass, then add mineral water or champagne. Drink will foam up, so pour slowly.

YIELDS: 1½ cups.

GOOD SOURCE OF: Beta-carotene, vitamin A, B-complex, C, D, E, and K; iron; calcium; sodium; potassium; magnesium; manganese; sulfur; copper; and phosphorus.

GOOD FOR: Constipation, general cleansing.

Virgin Mary

· ·

6 medium tomatoes
2 stalks celery
½ lemon, peeled but with white pith remaining
dash Tabasco (or more to taste)
pepper to taste
1 ounce vodka, optional

1. Cut tomatoes into wedges to fit into juicer. Juice and save pulp for pasta sauce or salsa.

2. Juice celery and lemon, and stir in other ingredients.

YIELDS: 2 cups.

GOOD SOURCE OF: Vitamin A, B1, B2, B6, C, and K; phosphorus; potassium; iron; bromine; sodium; magnesium; manganese; iodine; and copper.

GOOD FOR: Skin, general cleansing.

Hula Cooler

. . . .

3 pineapple spears
1 bunch red seedless grapes
¼ lemon, peeled but with white pith remaining
1 cup crushed ice
½ cup club soda
1 ounce either light or dark rum, optional
1 pineapple ring for garnish

1. Juice pineapple spears, freezing pulp for later use.
2. Juice grapes and lemon.
3. Pour over crushed ice; add club soda and rum, if desired.
4. Hang pineapple slice on edge of glass.

YIELDS: 2 cups.

GOOD SOURCE OF: Vitamin A, B-complex, and C; iodine; magnesium; manganese; potassium; calcium; phosphorus; iron; and sulfur.

GOOD FOR: Regularity, general cleansing.

Grapefruit Swirl

. . . .

3 pineapple spears
½ pink grapefruit, peeled but with white pith
  remaining
2 strawberries
1 banana
1 ounce rum, optional

1. Juice pineapple spears, freezing pulp for later use.
2. Juice grapefruit and strawberries.
3. Place broken-up banana in blender; add juice and rum, if desired; blend, pour, and drink.

YIELDS: 1½ cups.

GOOD SOURCE OF: Vitamin A, B-complex, C, E, and K; iron; sodium; phosphorus; magnesium; potassium; sulfur; calcium; silicon; iodine; and bromine.

GOOD FOR: Digestion, colds and flu.

Tropical Smoothie

. . . .

3 pineapple spears
½ papaya, peeled
1 kiwi fruit, unpeeled
1 ounce rum, optional

1. Juice pineapple spears, freezing pulp for later use.
2. Juice papaya and kiwi, freezing pulp for later use.
3. Add rum, if desired; stir and drink.

YIELDS: 1 cup.

GOOD SOURCE OF: Vitamin A, B-complex, and C; protein; iodine; magnesium; manganese; potassium; calcium; phosphorus; iron; and sulfur.

GOOD FOR: Ulcers, general cleansing.

Fizzy Georgia

. . . .

2 medium peaches
4 apricots
5 sweet cherries
5 ounces sparkling mineral water or
    champagne

1. Pit peaches, apricot, and cherries. If your juicer has trouble processing peach and apricot skins, peel peaches and apricots.

2. Put fruits through juicer, freezing pulp for sorbet.

3. Stir juice in large glass and slowly pour in mineral water or champagne. Drink will fizz up.

YIELDS: 1⅓ cups.

GOOD SOURCE OF: Vitamin A, B, and C; and protein.

GOOD FOR: Ulcers, cleansing bowels, cancer prevention.

June Punch
• •

1 pint strawberries, stems removed
½ pineapple, skin removed and cut into spears
2 pounds red grapes
2 ounces rum, optional

1. Juice strawberries and pineapple, saving pulp for Pine-Straw Topping.

2. Juice grapes.

3. Pour juices and rum, if desired, into pitcher and serve over ice.

YIELDS: 4 cups.

GOOD SOURCE OF: Vitamin A, B-complex, C, E, and K; iron; sodium; phosphorus; magnesium; potassium; sulfur; calcium; silicon; iodine; and bromine.

GOOD FOR: Skin, muscle soreness.

Not-So-Bloody Mary

. . . .

3 large carrots
2 stalks celery, 1½ to juice; reserve top ½ of
second for garnish
6 medium tomatoes
Tabasco sauce
2 ounces vodka, optional

1. Juice carrots and celery, saving pulp for Simple Carrot Cake.

2. Juice tomatoes, saving pulp for pasta sauce.

3. Mix all ingredients, including vodka, if desired, add Tabasco sauce to taste, and serve over ice, garnished with top half of celery stalk.

YIELDS: 3½ cups.

GOOD SOURCE OF: Vitamin A, B-complex, C, D, E, and K; phosphorus; potassium; iron; bromine; sodium; magnesium; manganese; sulfur; and copper.

GOOD FOR: Ulcers, cancer prevention.

Pineapple Fizz
. . . .

> 2 medium oranges, peeled but with white pith
>   remaining
> ¼ lime, peeled but with white pith remaining
> 2 cups pineapple pulp, frozen
> 6 ounces ginger ale or champagne

1. Stand blender next to juicer.
2. Juice oranges and lime.
3. Scoop frozen pineapple pulp into blender. Pour in citrus juices.
4. Blend at low speed.
5. Spoon into large glass, or divide between two medium glasses.
6. Pour in ginger ale or champagne.

YIELDS: 3½ cups.

GOOD SOURCE OF: Vitamin A, B-complex, C, and P; iodine; magnesium; manganese; potassium; calcium; phosphorus; iron; and sulfur.

GOOD FOR: Digestion, colds and flu.

Island Cooler

· ·

1 pineapple, skin removed, cut into spears
1 pint strawberries, stems removed
2 large sweet apples
3 ounces rum, optional

1. Juice pineapple and strawberries, saving pulp for Pine-Straw Topping.

2. Juice apples, saving pulp for applesauce.

3. Stir juices, pour into pitcher, and add rum, if desired. Serve over ice.

YIELDS: 6 cups.

GOOD SOURCE OF: Vitamin A, B-complex, C, E, and K; iodine; magnesium; manganese; potassium; calcium; phosphorus; iron; sulfur; sodium; silicon; and bromine.

GOOD FOR: Digestion, colds and flu.

Strawberry Special
. . . .

1 pint strawberries, stems removed
½ pint raspberries
½ lemon, peeled but with white pith remaining
20 ounces sparkling mineral water, champagne

1. Juice strawberries and raspberries, immediately freezing pulp for Berry Sorbet.

2. Juice lemon. Stir juices together in pitcher.

3. Add mineral water or champagne, if desired. Serve over ice.

YIELDS: 5 cups.

GOOD SOURCE OF: Vitamin A, B-complex, C, E, and K; iron; sodium; phosphorus; magnesium; potassium; sulfur; calcium; silicon; iodine; and bromine.

GOOD FOR: Skin, weight loss.

Equator Shake

. . . .

> ¼ *pineapple, skin removed, cut into spears*
> 1 *mango, peeled, cut into spears*
> 1 *medium tomato*
> 1½ *ounces rum, optional*

1. Juice pineapple and mango, immediately freezing pulp for Tropical Sorbet.

2. Juice tomato, saving pulp for pasta sauce.

3. Place all juices in a sealable container, add rum, if desired, seal, shake contents thoroughly, and pour into glasses.

YIELDS: 2 cups.

GOOD SOURCE OF: Vitamin A, B-complex, C, and K; iodine; magnesium; manganese; potassium; calcium; phosphorus; iron; sulfur; and bromine.

GOOD FOR Digestion, colds and flu.

Spicy Carrot Drink
. . . .

½ teaspoon cinnamon
½ teaspoon cardamom
4 medium carrots
1 Red or Golden Delicious apple
½ teaspoon ginger root
10 ounces sparkling mineral water or
    champagne

1. Sprinkle cinnamon and cardamom in juicer. Run carrots and ginger through, saving pulp for Simple Carrot Cake.
2. Run apple through, saving pulp for later use.
3. Pour into glasses and add mineral water or champagne.

YIELDS: 2½ cups.

GOOD SOURCE OF: Vitamin A, B-complex, C, D, E, and K; iron; calcium; sodium; potassium; magnesium; manganese; sulfur; copper; and phosphorus.

GOOD FOR: Ulcers, cancer prevention.

Apple Bubbler

. . . .

4 large apples
10 ounces sparkling mineral water or
  champagne

1. Juice apples, saving pulp for later use.
2. Pour mineral water or champagne into juice.

YIELDS: 3 cups.

GOOD SOURCE OF: Vitamin B1, B2, B6, and C; niacin; and trace minerals.

GOOD FOR: Skin and hair, detoxifying.

The Hawaiian Tourist

. . . .

1 papaya, peeled, and cut into spears
1 guava, meat separated from seed and skin
1 pineapple, skin removed, cut into spears
2 ounces rum, optional

1. Juice all fruits, immediately freezing pulp for Hawaiian Sorbet.
2. Stir thoroughly; pour rum over top, if desired, and serve.

YIELDS: 4 cups.

GOOD SOURCE OF: Vitamin A, B-complex, and C; iodine; magnesium; manganese; potassium; calcium; phosphorus; iron; sulfur; and protein.

GOOD FOR: Colds and flu, general cleanser.

Kiwi Cooler

· ·

6 large kiwi fruits
¼ lemon, peeled but with white pith remaining
12 ounces ginger ale or champagne

1. Juice kiwis and lemon, saving pulp for Kiwi Sorbet.
2. Add ginger ale or champagne.

YIELDS: 2 cups.

GOOD SOURCE OF: Vitamin A, C, and D; calcium; and phosphorus.

GOOD FOR: Skin, colds and flu.

Pomegranate Plus

· ·

8 large pomegranates, peeled
1 medium lemon, peeled but with white pith
*   remaining*
20 ounces sparkling mineral water or
*   champagne*

1. Juice pomegranates and lemon.
2. Stir juices thoroughly, add mineral water or champagne, and stir gently.

YIELDS: 4 cups.

GOOD SOURCE OF: Carbohydrates, vitamin A, C, and P; calcium; phosphorus; and potassium.

GOOD FOR: Colds and flu.

Piña Colada

. . . .

1 pineapple spear
2 ounces rum
½ cup crushed ice

1. Set blender next to juicer.
2. Juice pineapple spear. Dump both juice and pulp into blender. Add rum and ice. Blend for 10 seconds at slow speed.
3. Pour over ice.

YIELDS: ½ cup.

GOOD SOURCE OF: Vitamin A, B-complex, and C; iodine, magnesium; manganese, potassium; calcium, phosphorus; iron; and sulfur.

GOOD FOR: Digestion, colds and flu.

Screwdriver

. . . .

1 very ripe, very sweet orange, peeled but with
*   white pith remaining*
1½ ounces vodka

1. Juice orange.
2. Add vodka and stir.

YIELDS: ½ cup.

GOOD SOURCE OF: Vitamin A, C, and P; calcium; and phosphorus.

GOOD FOR: Digestion, colds and flu.

Exotic Cocktails

In "A Walk on the Wild Side," I urged you to experiment with some of the more unusual fruits and vegetables. Here are just a few more recipes to start you and your guests on your exotic adventures.

The Daikon Reactor
. . . .

> 1 medium leek
> 3 medium to large tomatillos
> ½ medium daikon radish
> ½ jicama
> 1 Belgian endive

1. Use lower third of leek, removing outer layer so as not to jam machine. Remove outer shells from tomatillos and wash. Wash radish. Slice jicama to fit juicer opening, but do not remove skin.
2. Feed all ingredients into juicer. Stir juice to mix.
3. Drink immediately, as this juice is tangy and strong and will not keep well.

YIELDS: 1 cup.

GOOD SOURCE OF: Vitamin A, B1, and C; calcium; potassium; phosphorus; and iron.

GOOD FOR: Regularity, colds and flu, general cleanser.

Papaya Surprise

. . . .

1 pineapple, skin removed, cut into spears
1 papaya, peeled, cut into spears

1. Juice pineapple spears, freezing pulp for later use.
2. Feed papaya into juicer, freezing pulp for later use.
3. Stir and drink straight or over ice.

YIELDS: 3 cups.

GOOD SOURCE OF: Vitamin A, B-complex, and C; iodine; magnesium; manganese; potassium; calcium; phosphorus; iron; and sulfur.

GOOD FOR: Ulcers, general cleanser.

Pine-Go

. . . .

4 pineapple spears
1 mango

1. Juice pineapple spears, freezing pulp for later use.
2. Slice mango in half lengthwise, twist apart over bowl (to catch juices), removing pit. Cut clinging pulp away from pit and juice meat. Scoop out remaining mango meat and process all meat, then run collected juice from bowl through juicer.
3. Stir and drink straight or over ice.

YIELDS: 1 cup.

GOOD SOURCE OF: Vitamin A, B-complex, and C; iodine; magnesium; manganese; potassium; calcium; phosphorus; iron; and sulfur.

GOOD FOR: Digestion, colds and flu.

Exotic Zinger

. . . .

1 tablespoon fresh cilantro
1 passion fruit, peeled
1 jalapeño pepper
6 sugar snap peas, strings removed
1 lime, peeled but with white pith remaining
1 medium cucumber, peeled

1. Place cilantro in juicer. Juice passion fruit, then add chili pepper.

2. Juice jalapeño and peas, then add lime and cucumber.

YIELDS: 1 cup.

GOOD SOURCE OF: Vitamin A, B-complex, and C; protein; iron; silicon; sulfur; manganese; potassium; sodium; calcium; and phosphorus.

GOOD FOR: Skin, colds and flu.

Party Time
. . . .

2 pounds carrots
¾ Chinese cabbage
1 bell pepper
1 red bell pepper
5 sweet apples
1 bunch celery
¾ pound spinach
¾ pound jicama
½ pound bok choy

1. Juice carrots and apples together and stir pulp for Apple-Carrot Sauce.

2. Juice all additional ingredients and stir thoroughly.

YIELDS: 1 quart.

GOOD SOURCE OF: Vitamin A, B-complex, C, D, E, and K; iron; calcium; sodium; potassium; magnesium; manganese; sulfur; copper; phosphorus; niacin; iodine; chlorophyll; and mucilage.

GOOD FOR: Eyes, skin, and hair, regularity, colds and flu, general cleanser.

Tropi-Dew

. . . .

½ *pineapple, skin removed, cut into spears*
1 *large orange, peeled but with white pith*
remaining
1 *papaya or 1 mango, peeled, pit or seeds*
removed
2 *large carrots*
½ *lime, peeled but with white pith remaining*

1. Juice pineapple and papaya or mango and lime together and use pulp for breakfast or dessert topping.
2. Juice carrots and save pulp for variety of uses.
3. Juice orange and mix all juices.

YIELDS: 4 cups.

GOOD SOURCE OF: Vitamin A, B-complex, C, D, E, and K; sodium; copper; iodine; magnesium; manganese; potassium; calcium; phosphorus; iron; and sulfur.

GOOD FOR: Eyes, ulcers and digestion, general cleanser, cancer prevention.

Pacific Paradise
• •

½ pineapple, skin removed, cut into spears
3 large kiwis, unpeeled
½ lime, peeled but with white pith remaining
½ lemon, peeled but with white pith remaining

1. Juice all ingredients, saving pulp for breakfast or dessert topping.
2. Stir juice and drink.

YIELDS: 3 cups.

GOOD SOURCE OF: Vitamin A, B-complex, and C; iodine; magnesium; manganese; potassium; calcium; phosphorus; iron; and sulfur.

GOOD FOR: Blood problems, colds and flu, digestion.

6

Baby Food and Pulp Recipes

Now we come to the marvelous fringe benefits of the juicing revolution—the healthful and appetizing foods you can make using the fruit and vegetable pulp from your juicing. This chapter presents recipes for everything from the freshest possible food for your baby to spicy salsas and delectable baked goods for you and your guests.

Fresh Baby Food

Because a baby has different nutritional needs from an adult, and because the baby's digestive system is more delicate, some precautions must be taken when making fresh juices and baby foods with your juicer.

Before juicing, all fruits and vegetables should be

washed thoroughly and peeled, and seeds and stems
should be removed. Fruits used for pure juice will process
out through the juice side of the machine. You can then
use the seeded, skinned pulp of apples, for instance, as
applesauce.

Fruits and vegetables that are to be used for baby
food should be lightly steamed for ten minutes before processing through your juicer. After you process steamed
fruits or vegetables, you will need to disassemble the machine and use a spatula to remove the baby food from the
upper part of the machine.

Instead of giving you specific recipes, this section
separates the baby foods into juices and solids. This will
give you the basics with which you can create an unlim-
ited variety of recipes.

Hints

Brenda Rodreques, my secretary and personal assistant,
as a new mother decided to save time by making her own
baby food in bulk. She poured the food she made in her
juicer into ice-cube trays, froze them, then stored the
cubes in freezer bags, and when she wanted to feed her
baby, she popped one or two cubes into the microwave to
thaw and served them. The amounts of juice or solid food
given below are approximate; you'll find that the yields
will vary according to the size, kind, and degree of ripeness of the fruit.

When using stringy vegetables (such as green beans),
first remove all the strings you can see; the vegetable will
then need to be run through the juicer at least twice,
mixing the juice and pulp on the second run-through. If
the food is still too thick, add 1 or 2 tablespoons of water.

Juices

Wash fruit thoroughly before processing. When using fresh apricots or peaches, remove the skins first, both because they can jam certain machines and because they are difficult for babies to digest.

1. Apple juice: 3 to 4 medium sweet apples yield 1 cup.
2. Pineapple-carrot juice: 2 carrots and 2 spears of pineapple yield 1 cup.
3. Orange juice: 2 medium oranges, skinned (but with white pith left on), yield 1 cup.
4. Orange-carrot juice: 1 skinned orange and 1 carrot yield ¾ cup.
5. Apple-carrot juice: 2 red apples and 1 carrot yield 1 cup.
6. Apple-grape juice: 2 apples and a small bunch of seedless grapes yield 1 cup.
7. Pear juice: 2 medium pears yield 1 cup.

Solids

Wash fruits and vegetables thoroughly; remove all skin, seeds, strings, and stems before lightly steaming (10 to 15 minutes). After processing through the machine, remove with a spatula from the inner top of the machine.

Be creative in combining solids. My son loved mixed mashed potatoes and mashed carrots. Your baby will let you know which of your combinations pleases.

1. Banana-pineapple sauce. These fruits do not need to be steamed before mixing. Mash 3 firm bananas and juice 7 spears of pineapple, saving

juice and mixing pulp with mashed bananas. Yields 1 cup.

2. Applesauce. Steam 3 medium red apples that have been skinned and seeded. Run through machine. Add touch of cinnamon. Yields 1 cup.

3. Mash 2 to 3 firm bananas or use a blender. Can be mixed with pulp produced by making juices from juice listed above. Yields 1 cup.

4. Pear sauce. Steam 2 medium pears that have been skinned and seeded. Run through machine. Add touch of cinnamon. Yields 1 cup.

5. Green beans. String beans before steaming. Steam for 15 minutes. Add 1 or 2 tablespoons water if beans come out too dry. 1 pound beans yields 1 cup.

6. Carrots. Three carrots yield 1 cup.

7. Peas. Peas are better for children one to two years old; younger children have trouble digesting them. When preparing peas, depod them first. Because of the differences among the types of peas, it is difficult to give a precise pounds-equals-cups formula, but a rule of thumb is 1 pound of peas yields about ½ cup.

8. Squash. Four zucchini or 4 yellow summer squash yield 1½ cups.

9. Sweet potato. Potatoes take longer to steam than other vegetables; sweet potatoes should be steamed 20 to 25 minutes. A large sweet potato yields 1 cup.

10. Beets. Four medium peeled beets (add a spear of uncooked pineapple to sweeten) yield 2 cups.

No-Waste Cooking and Baking

For some of these recipes, especially those which use fruit pulp, you need to immediately freeze the pulp from your juicing to preserve its freshness. For other recipes (such as the ones which use carrot pulp), you can collect the pulp in a sealed plastic or glass container, and store for one or two days in your refrigerator.

Some pulp (such as cabbage) should be used immediately for such recipes as cole slaw, salad topping, or soup, since processed cabbage alone does not keep well.

Soups

Quick Veggie Soup
. . . .

> 4 stalks celery
> 4 medium carrots
> 2 medium zucchini
> 1 small onion

1. Juice all ingredients.
2. Pour juice and pulp into pan, heat, and serve.

YIELDS: 1 cup.

GOOD SOURCE OF: Beta-carotene; vitamin A, B-complex, C, D, E, and K; iron; calcium; sodium; potassium; magnesium; manganese; sulfur; copper; phosphorus; iodine; bactericides.

GOOD FOR: Ulcers, general cleansing.

Simple Soup

. . . .

1 medium can (14 ounces) chicken broth
1 cup carrot pulp
½ cup beet pulp
½ cup summer or winter squash pulp

Pour all ingredients into pot, simmer, and stir until hot.

YIELDS: 3 cups.

GOOD SOURCE OF: Vitamin A, B-complex, C, D, E, and K; potassium; magnesium; phosphorus; sulfur; iron; calcium; sodium; manganese; and copper.

GOOD FOR: Urinary tract, cancer prevention.

Blender Soup

. . . .

1 medium can (14 ounces) chicken broth
Pulp of 2 carrots
Pulp of 1 zucchini
Pulp of 1 medium bell pepper
Pulp of 2 stalks celery

1. Mix all ingredients in blender.
2. Pour into saucepan and bring to boil.

YIELDS: 2 cups.

GOOD SOURCE OF: Beta-carotene; vitamin A, B-complex, C, D, E, and K; iron; calcium; sodium; potassium; magnesium; manganese; sulfur; copper; phosphorus; and iodine.

GOOD FOR: Ulcers, cancer prevention.

Carrot-Raisin-Pineapple Salad
· ·

2 cups carrot pulp
½ cup raisins or currants
½ cup pineapple pulp
¼ cup honey
¼ cup canola oil
Juice of ¼ lemon
¼ cup chopped walnuts
Lettuce leaves

1. Toss all ingredients except lettuce together until thoroughly mixed.
2. Serve on lettuce leaves.

YIELDS: 3½ cups.

GOOD SOURCE OF: Beta-carotene; vitamin A, B-complex, C, D, E, K, and P; iron; calcium; sodium; potassium; magnesium; manganese; sulfur; copper; phosphorus; and iodine.

GOOD FOR: Ulcers, colds and flu, cancer prevention.

White Radish and Jicama Salad

. . . .

1 cup white radish pulp
¼ cup carrot pulp
¼ cup jicama pulp
Lettuce leaves
1 cucumber, unpeeled
Dressing of your choice

1. Arrange pulped vegetables on lettuce leaves in layers.
2. Slice cucumbers and arrange around plate.
3. Top with your favorite dressing.

YIELDS: 1½ cups.

GOOD SOURCE OF: Beta-carotene; vitamin A, B-complex, C, D, E, K, and P; iron; calcium; sodium; potassium; magnesium; sulfur; manganese; copper; phosphorus; iodine; and silicon.

GOOD FOR: General cleanser.

Pasta Salad

. . . .

1 12-ounce bag rotini pasta
2 tablespoons cauliflower pulp
2 tablespoons carrot pulp
2 tablespoons celery pulp
2 tablespoons broccoli pulp
½ teaspoon pepper
½ teaspoon garlic powder
1 teaspoon parsley
1 small bottle fat-free Italian dressing

1. Cook pasta ahead of time and chill.
2. Add the rest of the ingredients except the dressing and mix together.
3. Mix in Italian dressing and serve.

YIELDS: 4 cups.

GOOD SOURCE OF: Beta-carotene; vitamin A, B-complex, C, D, E, and K; sodium; magnesium; manganese; iron; iodine; copper; potassium; calcium; phosphorus; and riboflavin.

GOOD FOR: Eyes and skin, ulcers and digestion, gout, allergies, anemia and arthritis, general cleansing, cancer prevention.

Side Dishes

Tomato Stuffed with Broccoli

· ·

> 1 tomato
> ½ cup broccoli pulp per serving
> Onion powder and/or garlic powder to taste
> Grated cheese of your choice

1. Core tomato.
2. Steam broccoli pulp for 5 minutes and add onion and/or garlic powder to taste.
3. Stuff tomato with broccoli mixture.
4. Top with grated cheese.
5. Place in oiled baking dish under broiler and broil until heated through.

YIELDS: 1 stuffed tomato.

GOOD SOURCE OF: Vitamin A, B1, B2, B6, C, and K; phosphorus; potassium; iron; bromine; and calcium.

GOOD FOR: General cleanser, cancer prevention.

Cole Slaw

. . . .

3 cups cabbage pulp
1½ cups carrot pulp
1 tablespoon white vinegar
3 tablespoons reduced-calorie mayonnaise
Parlsey sprig for garnish

1. Mix together cabbage and carrot pulp.
2. Stir in vinegar and mayonnaise until thoroughly mixed.
3. Garnish with parsley sprig.

YIELDS: 4½ cups.

GOOD SOURCE OF: Beta-carotene; vitamin A, B-complex, C, D, E, and K; iron; calcium; sodium; potassium; magnesium; manganese; sulfur; copper; phosphorus; and iodine.

GOOD FOR: Ulcers, cancer prevention.

Veggie Chili

. . . .

1 pound dried kidney beans
7 cups water
½ cup zucchini pulp
⅓ cup onion pulp
½ cup bell pepper pulp
1 cup tomato pulp
4 garlic cloves
1 tablespoon chili powder
1 tablespoon basil
½ tablespoon oregano
1 teaspoon pepper
2 teaspoons salt
1 teaspoon cumin
1½ cups tomato juice

1. Soak kidney beans overnight.
2. Drain and replace water. Add all ingredients to beans and simmer for 4 hours.

YIELDS: 8 servings.

GOOD SOURCE OF: Vitamin A, B1, B2, B6, C, and K; phosphorus; potassium; iron; bromine; and bactericides.

GOOD FOR: Skin, blood pressure, general cleansing.

Stuffed Zucchini
· ·

1 cup uncooked brown rice
2 cups tomato pulp
2 tablespoons onion pulp
1 tablespoon parsley
2 garlic cloves
¼ teaspoon pepper
½ teaspoon salt
1 large zucchini

1. Cook rice per directions and mix with remaining ingredients except zucchini. Preheat oven to 350°.

2. Slice zucchini in half lengthwise, scooping out insides.

3. Fill zucchini with rice mixture and bake for 1 hour.

Note: For a more Italian taste, add more tomato pulp with juice, rosemary, sage, and garlic.

YIELDS: 2 servings.

GOOD SOURCE OF: Vitamin A, B1, B2, B6, C, and K; phosphorus; potassium; iron; bromine; sodium; calcium; magnesium; sulfur; manganese; copper; and iodine

GOOD FOR: Skin, circulation, general cleansing.

Salsas and Dips

Tomato Yogurt Dip
. . . .

1 cup tomato pulp
¼ cup horseradish
2 tablespoons onion pulp
½ cup plain low-fat yogurt

1. Mix tomato pulp, horseradish, and onion pulp.
2. Fold in yogurt.
3. Serve with assorted raw vegetables (cauliflower, broccoli, carrots, celery, jicama, etc.).

YIELDS: 1¾ cups.

GOOD SOURCE OF: Vitamin A, B1, B2, B6, C, and K; phosphorus; potassium; iron; bromine; and bactericides.

GOOD FOR: Skin, general cleansing.

Simple Salsa
• •

> 2 cups tomato pulp
> ¼ cup onion pulp
> 1 teaspoon cilantro pulp

Mix all ingredients and serve with chips or raw vegetables.

YIELDS: 1¼ cups.

GOOD SOURCE OF: Vitamin A, B1, B2, B6, C, and K; phosphorus; potassium; iron; and bromine.

GOOD FOR: Skin, general cleanser.

Salsa Salsa
• •

> All ingredients are produced by making Tomato
>   Salsa Drink.
> Tomato pulp
> Jalapeño pepper pulp
> Onion pulp
> Cilantro pulp
> Lime pulp

Collect pulps from Tomato Salsa Drink recipe, stir together, chill, and serve with chips or vegetables.

YIELDS: ½ cup.

GOOD SOURCE OF: Vitamin A, B1, B2, B6, C, and K; phosphorus; potassium; iron; and bromine.

GOOD FOR: Skin, general cleanser.

Zippy Salsa Dip

. . . .

2 cups tomato pulp and juice
½ large onion
1 teaspoon fresh cilantro
1 clove garlic
1 jalapeño pepper, sliced

1. Run all ingredients through juicer.
2. Combine all ingredients, juice and pulp. Stir and serve with chips or vegetables.

YIELDS: 2½ cups.

GOOD SOURCE OF: Vitamin A, B1, B2, B6, C, and K; phosphorus; potassium; iron; bromine; bactericides; and fiber.

GOOD FOR: Skin, general cleanser.

Citrus Salsa

·······································

3 medium tomatoes
1 lemon, peeled but with white pith remaining
1 clove garlic
2 fresh jalapeño peppers
1 small red onion

1. Juice tomatoes, lemon, onion, garlic, and peppers. (For crunchier salsa, chop onions.)

2. Combine all juice and pulp, stir, and serve with chips or vegetables.

YIELDS: 1 cup.

GOOD SOURCE OF: Vitamin A, B1, B2, B6, C, and K; phosphorus; potassium; iron, bromine; bactericides; and fiber.

GOOD FOR: Colds and flu, skin.

Spicy Tomato Dressing

. . . .

6 medium ripe tomatoes, peeled
⅛ cup cider vinegar
⅛ cup canola oil
1 tablespoon Worcestershire sauce
⅛ teaspoon pepper
1 tablespoon honey
1 teaspoon dry mustard
2 tablespoons minced garlic

1. Run tomatoes through juicer twice. Use all pulp and juice.
2. Add remaining ingredients, stir, and serve over salad or as a vegetable dip.

YIELDS: 2 cups.

GOOD SOURCE OF: Vitamin A, B1, B2, B6, C, and K; phosphorus; potassium; iron; bromine; bactericides; and fiber.

GOOD FOR: Skin, digestion.

Spinach Dip
· ·

1 cup plain yogurt
¼ cup fat-free mayonnaise
1½ cups spinach pulp
½ cup parsley pulp (remove stems)
½ cup onion pulp
1 teaspoon salt
¼ teaspoon pepper
¼ teaspoon celery salt
1 round loaf French bread

1. Mix all ingredients except bread together and refrigerate overnight.

2. Hollow out French bread and place spinach dip inside.

3. Serve with veggies or pieces of bread.

GOOD SOURCE OF: Vitamin A, B-complex, and C; potassium; calcium; iron; phosphorus; magnesium; sulfur; manganese; zinc; copper; iodine; chlorophyll; sodium; and mucilage.

GOOD FOR: Skin, ulcers, digestion, and blood pressure, general cleansing, cancer and infection prevention.

Ham Glaze

∙∙

½ cup pineapple pulp
1 tablespoon honey

Mix both ingredients together.

GOOD SOURCE OF: Vitamin A, B-complex, and C; iodine; magnesium; manganese; potassium; calcium; phosphorus; iron; and sulfur.

GOOD FOR: Digestion; colds and flu.

Sweet and Sour Sauce

∙∙

1 cup malt vinegar
½ cup honey
1½ teaspoons salt
½ cup orange juice
½ cup pineapple juice
½ cup tomato pulp

Mix all ingredients together in a saucepan, bring to a boil, then simmer until thickened.

GOOD SOURCE OF: Vitamin A, B-complex, C, K, and P; iodine; magnesium; manganese; potassium; iron; sulfur; calcium; phosphorus; and bromine.

GOOD FOR: Skin, kidneys, bladder, liver, and gallbladder; colds and flu; digestion.

Main Dishes

Quick and Light Pasta Sauce
....

> 1½ cups yellow summer squash pulp
> 2 cups tomato pulp
> ½ cup beet or carrot pulp
> 1 tablespoon parsley
> ½ teaspoon dill weed
> 1 tablespoon pureed garlic
> ½ teaspoon ground pepper
> 1½ cups water
> 2 ounces celery juice

1. Combine all ingredients except water and celery juice.

2. When ingredients are thoroughly mixed, add water and celery juice, and stir slowly over low heat for 20 to 30 minutes.

3. When sauce is hot and well mixed, serve over pasta or use as topping on pizza crust or French bread.

YIELDS: 5½ cups.

GOOD SOURCE OF: Beta-carotene; vitamin A, B1, B2, B6, C, and K; phosphorus; potassium; iron; bromine; sulfur; calcium; magnesium; manganese; copper; and iodine.

GOOD FOR: General cleanser, cancer prevention.

Rich's Pasta Sauce

. . . .

¼ cup olive oil
1 teaspoon garlic puree or pulp
6 to 8 sliced mushrooms, optional
½ sliced large onion, optional
½ pound ground turkey
1 15-ounce can tomato sauce
2 cups tomato pulp
½ cup carrot pulp
25 anise seeds
2 tablespoons Italian seasoning
½ teaspoon dill weed

1. Pour olive oil into large pot; add garlic and brown over low heat. Add mushrooms and/or onions, if desired.

2. In a frying pan, brown and crumble ground turkey, pouring off liquid.

3. To oil and garlic add tomato sauce, tomato pulp, carrot pulp, and seasonings.

4. When sauce mixture warms, add ground turkey.

5. Simmer for 1 hour. Serve on spaghetti or other pasta.

YIELDS: 5 cups.

GOOD SOURCE OF: Beta-carotene; vitamin A, B-complex, C, D, E, and K; iron; calcium; sodium; potassium; magnesium; manganese; sulfur; copper; phosphorus; bromine; protein; and bactericides.

GOOD FOR: General cleanser, cancer prevention.

Beans with Peppers and Carrots

• •

4 cups water
2 cups dried lima beans
1 teaspoon sea salt
½ teaspoon pepper
½ teaspoon garlic powder
2 tablespoons safflower oil
Parsley sprig for garnish
Pulp of 1 medium onion
Pulp of ½ green bell pepper
Pulp of ½ red bell pepper
Pulp of 2 medium carrots

1. Boil water. Add beans, seasonings, oil, and onions. Cover and simmer for 1½ hours, adding more water if necessary.

2. Add pulp of bell peppers and carrots and simmer until pulp is tender.

YIELDS: 7 cups.

GOOD SOURCE OF: Beta-carotene; vitamin A, B-complex, C, D, E, and K; iron; calcium; sodium; potassium; magnesium; manganese; sulfur; copper; phosphorus; and bactericides.

GOOD FOR: Ulcers, lowering blood pressure.

Potato-Apple Pancakes

. . . .

1½ cups skim milk
Pulp of 8 medium potatoes
Pulp of 2 medium apples
4 egg whites, beaten
½ cup whole-grain flour
1½ teaspoons sea salt
½ teaspoon pepper
Canola oil for frying
Parsley sprig for garnish

1. Pour milk into large mixing bowl. Add potato pulp and mix.

2. In separate bowl, mix all other ingredients except oil and parsley. Blend thoroughly.

3. Pour contents of second bowl into first and mix together.

4. Pour canola oil into deep frying pan to depth of ½ inch and heat.

5. Drop about 3 tablespoons of batter into pan to make pancakes of whatever size you desire.

6. Press down on cakes with spatula and brown, turning, until crisp on both sides.

7. Drain on paper towels.

8. Serve pancakes with applesauce as side dish or topping. Garnish with parsley sprig.

YIELDS: 1 dozen medium pancakes.

GOOD SOURCE OF: Vitamin B-complex, C, and K; iron; phosphorus; protein; carbohydrates; sodium; calcium; magnesium; phosphorus; manganese; sulfur; and iodine.

GOOD FOR: Ulcers, general cleansing.

Turkey Loaf Surprise
. . . .

2 pounds ground turkey
1 cup bread crumbs
½ cup carrot pulp
½ cup onion pulp
1 nearly ripe banana, sliced
2 egg whites
2 tablespoons Italian seasoning
1 tablespoon mustard of your choice

1. Preheat oven to 350°.
2. Mix together all ingredients in bowl. Be sure banana is evenly distributed.
3. Form into loaf and place in greased baking dish.
4. Bake for 90 minutes.

YIELDS: 1 loaf that serves 6 to 8.

GOOD SOURCE OF: Beta-carotene; vitamin A, B-complex, C, D,
E, and K; iron; calcium; sodium; potassium; magnesium;
manganese; sulfur; copper; phosphorus; and bactericides.

GOOD FOR: Eyes and skin, ulcers and digestion, general
cleansing, cancer prevention.

Bob and Joe's Catch 'n' Bake

· ·

> 4 fish fillets (about 1 pound)
> 2 tablespoons fat-free mayonnaise
> 1 tablespoon onion pulp
> ½ teaspoon garlic powder
> salt and pepper to taste
> ½ cup tomato pulp
> ½ lemon

1. Preheat oven to 350°. Lay fish fillets in casserole dish. Cover fish with mayonnaise.

2. Spread on onion pulp, then sprinkle with garlic powder, salt, and pepper.

3. Cover fish with tomato pulp and squeeze juice of ½ lemon over all and cover with foil.

4. Bake for 15 minutes.

YIELDS: 4 servings.

GOOD SOURCE OF: Vitamin A, B1, B2, B6, C, and K; phosphorus; potassium; iron; bromine.

GOOD FOR: Skin, bladder, kidneys, gallbladder, liver.

Tuna Salad
· ·

1 6⅛-ounce can solid white tuna in spring
  water
¼ teaspoon pepper
2 tablespoons celery pulp
1 teaspoon onion pulp
½ teaspoon parsley
3 tablespoons fat-free mayonnaise
1 large ripe tomato

1. In large bowl, mix tuna, pepper, celery pulp, onion pulp, and parsley.

2. Add mayonnaise and mix again until thoroughly combined.

3. Stuff mixture into cored tomato.

Variation: Spread tuna salad on whole-wheat bread.

YIELDS: 1 serving.

GOOD SOURCE OF: Vitamin A, B-complex, C, and K; sodium; magnesium; manganese; iron; iodine; copper; potassium; calcium; phosphorus; bromine.

GOOD FOR: Teeth, bladder, kidneys, gallbladder, ulcers, general cleansing.

Stuffed Bell Peppers

. . . .

1 cup uncooked brown rice
¼ teaspoon parsley
1 tablespoon onion pulp
1 tablespoon celery pulp
1½ cups yellow squash pulp
½ teaspoon salt
½ teaspoon pepper
½ teaspoon garlic, minced
4 small bell peppers

1. Preheat oven to 350°. Cook rice per directions and set aside, covered.
2. Mix together parsley, onion pulp, celery pulp, yellow squash pulp, salt, pepper, and garlic.
3. Add rice to pulp mixture and stuff into small cored bell peppers.
4. Place on a baking sheet and cover with foil. Bake for 1 hour.

YIELDS: 4 servings.

GOOD SOURCE OF: Beta-carotene; vitamin A, B-complex, and C; sodium; potassium; calcium; iron; phosphorus; magnesium; sulfur; manganese; copper; and iodine.

GOOD FOR: Eyes, skin, and blood pressure; general cleanser.

Oat Bran Pizza Dough

· ·

1 cup warm water
1 package active dry yeast
3 to 4 cups oat bran flour
2 tablespoons olive oil
½ teaspoon salt

1. Combine the water, yeast, and 1½ cups oat bran flour in a large bowl. Mix well.

2. Add oil, salt, and the remaining flour (enough so the dough is just beyond sticky). Work all ingredients together using your hands.

3. On a lightly floured surface, knead dough until it is smooth and elastic. If the dough is still too wet, add a little more oat bran flour.

4. Put the dough in a lightly oiled bowl, cover with a towel or saran wrap, and place in a warm, sunny area. Let dough rise about 1 hour or until double in size.

5. When dough has risen sufficiently, roll it out on a lightly floured surface until it is ¼ inch thick.

6. Preheat over to 450°.

7. Top with Tomato Pulp Pizza Sauce and pizza toppings (recipes follow). Bake for 20 minutes or until crust is golden brown.

YIELD: 1 pizza shell.

GOOD SOURCE OF: Fiber; complex carbohydrates.

GOOD FOR: Regularity.

Tomato Pulp Pizza Sauce

. . . .

Pulp from 15 Roma tomatoes
2 large garlic cloves, minced
1½ teaspoons oregano
1 teaspoon dried sweet basil
1 bay leaf
fresh ground pepper to taste
¼ teaspoon salt

1. Bring tomato pulp to a boil. Reduce heat and simmer.

2. Add all other ingredients. Continue to simmer for 30 minutes, stirring occasionally.

3. Spread onto Oatbran Pizza Dough. Don't spread on too thick a layer because some may seep through crust.

YIELD: 1½ to 2 cups

GOOD SOURCE OF: Vitamin A, B1, B2, B6, C, and K; phosphorus; potassium; iron; bromine; and bactericides.

GOOD FOR: Skin, bladder problems, gallbladder problems, liver, kidneys, constipation, colds and flu.

Sausage and Mushroom Topping
· ·

1 pound Italian turkey sausage
10 large mushrooms, sliced and sauteed
½ cup grated Parmesan cheese

Spread sausage and mushrooms over sauce on pizza dough. Sprinkle with Parmesan cheese.

Seafood Specialty
· ·

3 ounces imitation crab
15 medium peeled and deveined butterfly
    shrimp, cooked
½ cup grated Parmesan cheese

Spread crab and shrimp over sauce on pizza dough. Sprinkle with Parmesan cheese.

Vegetarian
· ·

10 large mushrooms, sliced and sauteed
15 broccoli flowerets
1 large bell pepper, julienned
½ cup grated Parmesan cheese

Spread mushrooms, broccoli, and bell pepper evenly over sauce on pizza dough. Sprinkle with Parmesan cheese.

Spanish Omelet

2 egg whites
1 egg
Salt and pepper to taste
¼ cup tomato pulp
¼ cup bell pepper pulp
2 tablespoons onion pulp
½ teaspoon cilantro pulp

1. Spray nonstick frying pan with vegetable oil.
2. Mix eggs, salt, pepper. Pour mixture into pan and cook over low heat without stirring until omelet starts to bubble around edges. Cook until the bottom is set but the top is still slightly wet.
3. Mix one-half the tomato, bell pepper, onion, and cilantro pulps, then spread the mixture over one-half of the omelet and fold over the other half. Cook until filling is heated through, about 2 minutes.
4. Slide the omelet onto a plate, then heat remaining mixture in pan until hot and pour over top of omelet. Serve immediately.

YIELDS: 1 omelet.

GOOD SOURCE OF: Vitamin A, B1, B2, B6, C, and K; phosphorus; potassium; iron; and bromine.

GOOD FOR: Skin, bladder, gallbladder, liver, and kidneys.

Zucchini Omelet

. . . .

2 egg whites
1 egg
Salt and pepper to taste
¼ cup yellow squash pulp
¼ cup zucchini squash pulp
1 tablespoon parsley pulp (remove stems)
¼ teaspoon garlic puree

1. Spray nonstick frying pan with vegetable oil.
2. Mix together eggs and ¼ teaspoon each salt and pepper. Pour mixture into pan and cook over low heat without stirring until omelet starts to bubble around the edges. Cook until the bottom is set but the top is still slightly wet.
3. Mix squash, parsley, and garlic and spread over half the omelet, then fold the other half over it. Cook until filling is heated through, about 2 minutes.
4. Slide the omelet onto a plate, then sprinkle remaining salt and pepper over the top. Serve immediately.

YIELDS: 1 omelet.

GOOD SOURCE OF: Vitamin A, B-complex, and C; potassium; magnesium; sodium; calcium; iron; phosphorus; sulfur; manganese; copper; and iodine.

GOOD FOR: Eyes, anemia, gout, headaches, rheumatism, general cleansing.

Chicken with Red Pepper Pulp

2 boneless chicken breasts, skin removed
Pulp from 2 red bell peppers
1 garlic clove, minced
Pulp from 1 medium yellow squash
1 teaspoon vegetable seasoning
Pepper to taste

1. Preheat oven to 350°. Place chicken breasts in a sauce-pan. Cover with red pepper pulp, garlic, yellow squash pulp, vegetable seasoning, and pepper.
2. Cover with foil and bake for 1 hour.

GOOD SOURCE OF: Vitamin A, and C; potassium; magnesium; and bactericides.

GOOD FOR: Skin, heart, kidneys, and bladder, colds and flu, regularity, lowering blood pressure, and cancer prevention.

Salsa Chicken

· · · · · · · · · · · · · · · · · ·

2 boneless chicken

½ cup tomato pulp

¼ cup bell pepper pulp

1 tablespoon onion pulp

1 garlic clove, minced

1 tablespoon cilantro pulp

¼ cup red bell pepper pulp

¼ teaspoon salt

½ teaspoon cumin

2 tablespoons red wine vinegar

1. Preheat oven to 350°. Place chicken i   c
baking pan.

2. Mix remaining ingredients and pour over c

3. Cover with foil and bake for 1 hour.

GOOD SOURCE OF: Vitamin A, B1, B2, B6, C, and K; phosprus; potassium; iron; bromine; and bactericides.

GOOD FOR: Skin, bladder, gall bladder, liver, kidneys, and flu.

...ach Quiche

. . . .

cups spinach pulp
tablespoons carrot pulp
tablespoon onion pulp
½ teaspoon garlic powder
4 tablespoons margarine
4 tablespoons whole-wheat flour
1½ cups milk substitute
3 eggs
1 9-inch unbaked whole-wheat pie shell

1. Preheat oven to 375°. Mix spinach, carrot pulp, onion pulp, and garlic powder and set aside.
2. Melt margarine and add flour until smooth. Remove from heat. Add milk gradually (so it doesn't curdle) and eggs one at a time.
3. Add vegetable mixture and pour into pie crust.
4. Bake for 40 minutes.

YIELDS: 1 quiche; serves 6.

GOOD SOURCE OF: Vitamin A, B-complex, C, D, E, and K; sodium; potassium; calcium; iron; phosphorus; magnesium; sulfur; manganese; zinc; copper; iodine; chlorophyll; and mucilage.

GOOD FOR: Skin, ulcers, lowering blood pressure, regularity, general cleansing, cancer prevention.

Baked Goods

Summer Squash Loaf

. . . .

1½ cups yellow squash pulp
1½ cups mashed or minced dates
½ cup canola oil
4 egg whites
2½ teaspoons vanilla
2 cups whole-grain flour
½ teaspoon baking soda
1 teaspoon baking powder
2 teaspoons cinnamon

1. Preheat oven to 350°. In a bowl, beat squash and dates until mixed. Add oil slowly and mix well.

2. Continue to beat, gradually adding egg whites and vanilla.

3. Sift together dry ingredients.

4. Add combined dry ingredients to squash mixture. Stir gently until blended.

5. Pour into greased 9 × 5-inch loaf pan.

6. Bake for 1 hour.

YIELDS: 1 loaf.

GOOD SOURCE OF: Beta-carotene; vitamin A and C; potassium; magnesium; calcium; phosphorus; iron; and sodium.

GOOD FOR: Colds and flus, general cleanser.

Simple Carrot Cake
. . . .

1 cup canola oil
3½ cups carrot pulp
½ cup apple pulp
1 cup honey
6 egg whites
1 tablespoon vanilla
3 cups whole-grain flour
1 tablespoon baking soda
2 tablespoons cinnamon
2 teaspoons nutmeg
1½ cups crushed nuts

1. Preheat oven to 350°. Mix oil, carrot pulp, and apple pulp.
2. Add honey, egg whites, and vanilla and blend well.
3. Sift together dry ingredients, then add to mixture and stir until well blended.
4. Add nuts.
5. Pour into a greased 8½ × 4½ × 2½-inch pan.
6. Bake for 1 hour.

YIELDS: 1 cake.

GOOD SOURCE OF: Beta-carotene; vitamin A, B-complex, C, D, E, and K; iron; calcium; sodium; potassium; magnesium; manganese; sulfur; copper; phosphorus; and niacin.

GOOD FOR: Ulcers, cancer prevention.

Carrot-Pineapple Muffins

. . . .

3½ cups carrot pulp
1 cup pineapple pulp
1 cup honey
6 egg whites
1 cup canola oil
1 tablespoon vanilla
3 cups whole-grain flour
1 tablespoon baking soda
2 tablespoons cinnamon
1 teaspoon nutmeg
1½ cups crushed nuts

1. Preheat oven to 350°. Mix carrot and pineapple pulp.

2. Add honey, egg whites, oil, and vanilla and blend into mix.

3. Sift together dry ingredients and add to mixture, stirring until blended.

4. Add nuts.

5. Pour into muffin papers or greased muffin cups, filling three-quarters full.

6. Bake for 45 minutes.

YIELDS: 1 dozen muffins.

GOOD SOURCE OF: Beta-carotene; vitamin A, B-complex, C, D, E, and K; iron; calcium; sodium; potassium; magnesium; manganese; sulfur; copper; phosphorus; and iodine.

GOOD FOR: Colds and flu, cancer prevention.

Onion Bread

. . . .

1¾ cups milk substitute

4 tablespoons margarine

2 tablespoons honey

½ teaspoon celery salt

2 cups onion pulp

2 packages active dry yeast

½ cup water

½ teaspoon sage

6½ cups whole-wheat flour

1. Preheat oven to 350°. Heat milk substitute and 2 tablespoons of the margarine until scalding hot. Add honey and salt. Let cool.

2. Sauté onion pulp in the remaining margarine until brown.

3. Dissolve yeast in water and add to the cooled milk mixture.

4. Add sage to 2 cups of whole-wheat flour and mix.

5. Add the milk-yeast mixture and blend well. Add the onion pulp and the rest of the flour, and mix.

6. Place on a floured cutting board and knead until elastic.

7. Place in a bowl, cover, and let rise in a warm place until the mixture doubles in size.

8. Shape and place into 2 greased loaf pans, let rise again, and then bake for 50 minutes, or until golden brown.

YIELDS: 2 loaves.

GOOD SOURCE OF: Vitamin C; bactericides.

GOOD FOR: Colds and flu.

Zucchini Bread

. . . .

3 eggs
1 cup canola oil
1 cup honey
2 cups zucchini pulp
2 teaspoons baking soda
½ teaspoon baking powder
2 teaspoons salt
½ cup wheat germ
1½ cups oat flour
1 cup chopped walnuts

1. Preheat oven to 350°. Beat eggs.

2. Add oil and honey and beat until thick. Stir in zucchini pulp.

3. Add remaining ingredients and mix. Pour into 2 greased loaf pans.

4. Bake for 1 hour, or until golden brown.

YIELDS: 2 loaves.

GOOD SOURCE OF: Vitamin A, and C; potassium; and magnesium.

GOOD FOR: Kidneys and bladder, general cleansing.

Breakfast and Dessert Toppings

Apri-Cran Topping

. . . .

> ½ cup cranberry pulp
> ½ cup apricot pulp
> 2 tablespoons lemon pulp saved from Apri-Cran
> Juice

1. Keep mixed pulp chilled.
2. Use as topping for pancakes, waffles, or pound cake.

YIELDS: 1 cup.

GOOD SOURCE OF: Beta-carotene; vitamin A, B, C, and P; protein; calcium; and phosphorus.

GOOD FOR: Colds and flu, cancer prevention.

Vitamin C Punch Topping

. . . .

⅓ cup pineapple pulp
⅔ cup grapefruit pulp
2 tablespoons lemon pulp saved from Vitamin C
    Punch

Thoroughly mix ingredients, chill, and serve as pancake, waffle, or topping for pound cake or other dessert.

YIELDS: 1 cup.

GOOD SOURCE OF: Vitamin A, B-complex, C, and P; calcium; phosphorus; iodine; magnesium; manganese; potassium; iron; and sulfur.

GOOD FOR: Digestion, colds and flu.

Strawberry Topping

. . . .

Strawberry pulp saved from Summer Melon
    Medley

Chill strawberry pulp and use as pancake, waffle, or shortcake topping.

YIELDS: ¼ cup.

GOOD SOURCE OF: Vitamin B-complex, C, E, and K; iron; sodium; phosphorus; magnesium; potassium; sulfur; calcium; silicon; iodine; and bromine.

GOOD FOR: Skin, regularity.

Berry Blizzard Topping

½ cup cranberry pulp
½ cup raspberry pulp saved from Berry
    Blizzard

1. Thoroughly mix pulp and chill.
2. Serve as topping for pancakes, waffles, or frozen yogurt.

YIELDS: 1 cup.

GOOD SOURCE OF: Vitamin A, C, and P; calcium; and phosphorus.

GOOD FOR: Digestion, general cleanser.

Pine-Straw Topping

⅓ cup pineapple pulp
⅓ cup strawberry pulp saved from Pine-Straw
    Juice

1. Thoroughly mix pulp and chill.
2. Serve as topping for pancakes, waffles, or cake desserts.

YIELDS: ⅔ cup.

GOOD SOURCE OF: Vitamin A, B-complex, C, E, and I; iron; sodium; phosphorus; magnesium; potassium; sulfur; calcium; silicon; iodine; bromine; manganese; and sulfur.

GOOD FOR: Digestion, colds and flu.

Desserts

Apple Delight

· ·

> *1 cup apple pulp*
> *1 tablespoon lemon juice*
> *¼ cup raisins or sunflower seeds or a mixture of*
> *both*

1. Put apple pulp in small bowl. Add lemon juice and stir.
2. Top with raisins or sunflower seeds and serve.

YIELDS: 1 cup.

GOOD SOURCE OF: Vitamin B1, B2, B6, C, and P; niacin; calcium; and phosphorus.

GOOD FOR: Skin, hair, and detoxifying.

Tropical Sorbet

. . . .

¼ *pineapple pulp*
¼ *cup mango pulp saved from Equator Shake*

1. Thoroughly mix pulps and freeze in ice-cube tray.
2. When ready to make sorbet, take cubes from tray and run through juicer. Collect sorbet from pulp basket. Take machine apart to collect sorbet stuck to inside.

YIELDS: ½ cup.

GOOD SOURCE OF: Vitamin A, B-complex, C, and K; iodine; magnesium; manganese; potassium; calcium; phosphorus; iron; sulfur; and bromine.

GOOD FOR: Digestion, colds and flu.

Blackberry Applesauce

⅜ *cup apple pulp*
⅛ *cup blackberry pulp saved from Blackberry*
Apple Delight

1. Mix pulps thoroughly and chill.
2. Serve as dessert or side dish.

YIELDS: ½ cup.

GOOD SOURCE OF: Vitamin B1, B2, B6, and C; and niacin.

GOOD FOR: Skin, hair, and regularity.

Apple-Carrot Sauce

⅔ *cup apple pulp*
⅓ *cup carrot pulp*

Since apples and carrots are the stalwarts of any juicing program, you will undoubtedly collect quite a bit of both during a day. Chill pulps and at the end of the day blend them.

YIELDS: 1 cup.

GOOD SOURCE OF: Beta-carotene; vitamin A, B-complex, and C; sodium; magnesium; manganese; iron; iodine; copper; potassium; calcium; phosphorus; and niacin.

GOOD FOR: Skin, hair, and ulcers.

Hawaiian Sorbet

. . . .

½ cup papaya pulp
½ cup guava pulp
1 cup pineapple pulp saved from The Hawaiian
    Tourist

1. Freeze mixed pulp in ice-cube trays.
2. To make sorbet, run cubes through juicer and collect from pulp side. Take machine apart to scoop out excess sorbet.

YIELDS: 2 cups.

GOOD SOURCE OF: Vitamin A, B-complex, and C; iodine; magnesium; manganese; potassium; calcium; phosphorus; iron; sulfur; and protein.

GOOD FOR: Ulcers, general cleansing.

Carrot-Pineapple Sauce
. . . .

Pulp of 4 large carrots
Pulp of ¼ pineapple saved from Carrot Cake
    Juice
Parsley sprig for garnish

Stir pulps together and garnish with parsley sprig.

YIELDS: ½ cup.

GOOD SOURCE OF: Beta-carotene; vitamin A, B-complex, C, D,
E, and K; iron; calcium; sodium; potassium; magnesium;
manganese; sulfur; copper; phosphorus; and iodine.

GOOD FOR: Colds and flu, cancer prevention.

Kiwi Sorbet
. . . .

⅓ cup kiwi pulp
2 tablespoons lemon pulp saved from Kiwi
    Kooler

1. Freeze mixed pulp in ice-cube tray.
2. When ready to make sorbet, remove cubes and
run through juicer. Collect sorbet in pulp basket. Take
apart machine to scoop out clinging sorbet.

YIELDS: ⅓ cup.

GOOD SOURCE OF: Vitamin A, C, and P; calcium; and phosphorus.

GOOD FOR: Colds and flu and minor bruises.

Rasplesauce
....

Raspberry pulp saved from Raspberry Rush
1 cup apple pulp

Mix pulps and serve as dessert or side dish.

YIELDS: 1⅓ cups.

GOOD SOURCE OF: Vitamin A, B1, B2, B6, C, and P; niacin; calcium; and phosphorus.

GOOD FOR: Digestion and regularity.

Berry Sorbet
....

Strawberry pulp saved from Strawberry Special
Raspberry Pulp saved from Strawberry Special

1. Freeze mixed pulp in ice-cube tray.
2. When ready to use, extract ice cubes and run through juicer. Collect sorbet from pulp basket. Take machine apart to scoop out sorbet.

YIELDS: ½ cup.

GOOD SOURCE OF: Vitamin A, B-complex, C, E, and K; iron; sodium; phosphorus; magnesium; potassium; sulfur; calcium; silicon; iodine; and bromine.

GOOD FOR: Skin and sore muscles.

Pineapple Sauce
. . . .

Pineapple pulp saved from Pineapple Turbo

Chill and serve as dessert or side dish.

YIELDS: 1⅓ cups.

GOOD SOURCE OF: Vitamin A, B-complex, and C; iodine; magnesium; manganese; potassium; calcium; phosphorus; iron; and sulfur.

GOOD FOR: Digestion and colds and flu.

Apricot Whip
. . . .

1½ cups apricot pulp
1½ tablespoons lemon juice
⅓ cup honey
3 egg whites, beaten until they hold stiff peaks
Chopped nuts for garnish

1. Mix pulp, lemon juice, and honey.
2. Fold pulp mixture into beaten egg whites.
3. Serve with chopped nuts as garnish.

Note: Mixture can also be piled into an oiled baking dish and baked at 275°F for 30 to 35 minutes.

YIELDS: 3½ cups.

GOOD SOURCE OF: Beta-carotene; vitamin A, B, C, and P; protein; calcium; and phosphorus.

GOOD FOR: Colds and flu, and cancer prevention.

Melon Sorbet
. . . .

1-inch spears (without rind) of watermelon,
cantaloupe, honeydew, etc.

1. Freeze spears of one kind of melon or a variety of melons.
2. Partially thaw for about 5 minutes and process through juicer.
3. Scoop out sorbet from the pulp side. Take apart machine and scoop out sorbet. Serve immediately.

YIELDS: Approximately 1 cup per pound of frozen fruit.

GOOD SOURCE OF: Vitamin A, B, and C; cellulose; and essential fluids.

GOOD FOR: Skin, general cleansing.

Peachy Sorbet
. . . .

Peach, apricot, and cherry pulp saved from
Fizzy Georgia

1. Combine pulps and freeze in ice-cube tray.
2. Run ice cubes through juicer and collect as sorbet. Take machine apart to scoop out sorbet.

YIELDS: ½ cup.

GOOD SOURCE OF: Vitamin A, B, and C; and protein

GOOD FOR: Digestion, general cleanser.

Fruity Banana Split

. . . .

1 banana, cut in half lengthwise
1 scoop frozen pineapple pulp
1 scoop frozen watermelon pulp
1 scoop frozen cantaloupe pulp

1. Slit banana and lay in banana split dish.
2. Scoop in three frozen pulps.
3. (Optional) Top with pulp from various fruit juices: berries, cherries, etc.

YIELDS: 1 banana split.

GOOD SOURCE OF: Fiber; vitamin A, B-complex, and C; iodine; magnesium; manganese; potassium; phosphorus; iron; sulfur; and cellulose.

GOOD FOR: Digestion, colds and flu.

Brenda's Parfait
. . . .

Pineapple
Cantaloupe
Watermelon

1. Set out a dozen parfait glasses.
2. Juice enough pineapple spears to fill each of the first half dozen parfait glasses one-third full of juice. Freeze until solid. Use pineapple pulp to fill the bottom third of second half dozen glasses. Freeze.
3. Juice enough cantaloupe to fill second third of each parfait glass. Freeze. Use pulp to fill second half dozen glasses two-thirds full. Freeze.
4. Juice enough watermelon to fill first half dozen parfait glasses to the top. Freeze. Place pulp in second set of glasses. Freeze.
5. Serve as a dessert or palate-cleansing sorbet.

YIELDS: 3 cups.

GOOD SOURCE OF: Vitamin A, B-complex, and C; iodine; magnesium; manganese; potassium; calcium; phosphorus; iron; and sulfur.

GOOD FOR: Colds and flu, general cleansing.

Index

Acids, fruit, 61, 62, 64, 65
Activity
  juice recipes for, 37
  metabolism needs for, 36
  recommendations for, 36
Addititves in processed juice, 5
Advantages of juicing, 17
Aflatoxins. *See* Molds.
Aging
  diet supplements and, 32
  energy loss and, 32
  and juice needs, 30
  metabolism rate and, 32
  premature, x
  See also Older people;
    Seniors.
Alcohol, cancer risk and
    consumption of, 46
A. M. Blend, 112
Appetite stimulant, lemon as,
    29
Apple(s)
  Bubbler, 169
  Delight, 223
  juice for breakfast, 100
  juice, discussion of, 58
  juice as fruit juice staple, 58
  older people and, 33
  Pie Drink, 141
  Pucker, 132
  Turbo, 153
Apple-carrot-cucumber-broccoli
    juice, 117
Apple-carrot, pepper-jicama
    juice, 111
Apple-celery-spinach-parsley-
    Chinese cabbage juice,
    123
Apple-Potato Pancakes, 202

apple-vegetable juice, 122
Applesauce, Blackberry, 225
Apricot(s)
  baby food problems with,
    181
  juice, discussion of, 59
  Whip, 229
Apri-Cran
  Juice, 110
  Topping, 220
Artichoke juice, discussion of,
    69, 70
Asparagus juice, discussion of,
    70
Avocado juicing problems, 93

Baby
  food precautions, 179
  food recipes, 179
  food solids, 181
  juices, 181
Baked goods, 215
Banana
  juicing problems, 94
  Split, Fruity, 231
**Beans with Peppers and
    Carrots, 201**
Beet
  Goes On, The, 136
  juice, discussion of, 71
  Treat, 145
Belgian endive juice, 87
Berry
  Blizzard, 107
  Blizzard Topping, 223
  juice, discussion of, 59
  Sorbet, 228
Beta-Apple Lite, 145